Hollywood GANGSTERS

To Brigitte and Mandy, this book is dedicated.

GEOFF ANDREW

Hollywood GANGSTERS

GALLERY BOOKS
An Imprint of W. H. Smith Publishers Inc.
112 Madison Avenue
New York City 10016

Endpapers, left to right: Warren Oates in **Dillinger** (1973); Marilyn Monroe in **Some Like it Hot** (1959); Rod Steiger as **Al Capone** (1959); Shelley Winters in **Bloody Mama** (1970).

Page 1: Robert Mitchum in **The Friends of Eddie Coyle** (1973).

Pages 2-3: Three hoodlums are killed in **The St Valentine's Day Massacre** (1967).

Right: Popeye Doyle (Gene Hackman) in **The French Connection 2** (1976).

This book was devised and produced by Multimedia Publications (UK) Ltd

Editor: Richard Rosenfeld
Assistant Editor: Sydney Francis
Production: Karen Bromley
Design: John Strange and Associates
Picture Research: Veneta Bullen

First published in the United States of America 1985 by Gallery Books, an imprint of W. H. Smith Publishers Inc., 112 Madison Avenue, New York, NY 10016

ISBN 0 8317 4510 X

Typeset by Flowery
Origination by C.L.G. Verona
Printed in Italy by Sagdos, Milan

Note on titles and dates
US titles and release dates are used throughout.
*A few have had different titles for their original British release:
The Doorway to Hell (1930) – GB. A Handful of Clouds;
The Public Enemy (1931) – GB. Enemies of the Public;
The Whole Town's Talking (1935) – GB. Passport to Fame;
Roger Touhy, Gangster (1944) – GB. The Last Gangster;
The Enforcer (1951) – GB. Murder, Inc.;
Thief (1981) – GB. Violent Streets.

ACKNOWLEDGEMENTS
The views expressed in this history are my own and no other person should be blamed for them. Over years of movie-going and discussions, however, a large number of people have been helpful and influential regarding my ideas and the potential to express them. I should especially like to thank: David Thompson, Peter Howden, Tom Milne, Georges Meisner, Chris Peachment, Mick Eaton, Tony Rayns, Anne Billson, Martyn Auty, Rose Kenny, Carmel Kelly and Brigitte Cabos.

Contents

Eruptions in the Underworld 6
The Rise of the Mob 24
Rebels and Loners 46
The G-Men Fight Back 64
New Directions 80

Eruptions in the Underworld

A bullet in the arm marks the beginning of the end for Cesare Enrico Bandello, otherwise known as Rico. Edward G. Robinson's swarthy, almost Italianate looks served him well as **Little Caesar** (1930), one of the first great gangster movies.

I t is a dark and gloomy night. Inside a seedy, almost empty roadside diner Cesare "Rico" Bandello (Edward G. Robinson) and Joe Massara (Douglas Fairbanks Jr) are discussing their future careers in armed robbery. Rico is explaining to the more gentlemanly Joe the attraction of the criminal life: "Money's all right, but it ain't everything. No. Be somebody, know that a bunch of guys will do anythin' you tell 'em, have your own way or nothin' . . . 'Diamond Pete' Montana, he's somebody. And look at us, just a couple of nobodies."

It is characteristic of Hollywood's tendency to glamorize any movie hero – even a ruthless, vicious killer like Rico in Mervyn Le Roy's **Little Caesar** (1930) – that this up-and-coming mobster should give as the reason for his criminal ways not the incentive of money, but that of "being somebody". Cinema audiences have always been fascinated by how the other half lives, and hoodlums and killers have always been prime box-office fodder. But with the real-life impulse toward financial profit underplayed, Rico was not only endowed with his own perverse brand of dignity; he was also granted an acceptable quality. Particularly during the dismal years of the Depression, the average moviegoer could easily sympathize with the ambitious gangster's desire to climb the social and financial ladders and leave his mark on the world. Not surprisingly, **Little Caesar** was a huge and influential success.

Prohibition

Since the passing of the Volstead Act in 1919 introducing Prohibition, which made illegal the production, sale and transportation of alcoholic intoxicants, the American public had maintained a decidedly double-edged attitude towards gangsters. On the one hand, violence and murder were deplorable; on the other, Prohibition was a largely unpopular legal measure, and many regarded the racketeers' bootlegging of booze as a useful, necessary public service. Names like Al Capone and Hymie Weiss and Bugs Moran carried their own peculiar charisma, regarded by the American public with grudging admiration.

So, when in **Little Caesar** Rico made his meteoric rise to power over a city's criminal empire, he had little need to court sympathy from audiences all too willing to learn more about ruthless hoods and their illegal activities. Reflecting, loosely, the real-life career of Al Capone, and pursuing the ideals of the American Dream – power, fame, money, independence – Rico dazzled moviegoers with his boundless energy, streetwise

intelligence, and – despite his attempts at style – his ordinariness. He took obvious joy in the benefits of his trade – plush apartments, fine cars, flashy clothes – and yet when faced with a truly successful mobster ("The Big Boy", overall head of the city's crime force) Rico became disarmingly gauche, embarrassed, nervous.

On this level at least, Rico was certainly a figure to identify with. The audience could forgive his violence, partly because of the motivations behind it, partly because the victims are never innocents (it is only other criminals or cops who die), partly because Rico himself is finally killed, thanks to the censorious Hays Code's insistence that crime, in movies, should never pay. In fact, it is Rico's own pride and vanity that destroy him, not the forces of Law and Order; in response to allegations by the police (represented by relatively faceless and stilted individuals) that he is a chicken-hearted has-been, he comes out of hiding for one last showdown, only to be killed. The same violence, pride and ambition that drove him to the top of the heap are ultimately the cause of his downfall; as in a classical tragedy, the gangster hero carries within himself the seeds of his own destruction.

Rise of the urban criminal
Although **Little Caesar** is often claimed as the first real gangster movie, Hollywood had of course dealt with habitual, professional criminals before. As early as 1912 in a 15-minute short called **The Musketeers of Pig Alley**, pioneer director D. W. Griffith had shown waifish heroine Lillian Gish firmly resisting the advances of some gun-totin' unsavory types who occupied the grubby backstreets and smoky drinking haunts of New York's rough, tough Lower East Side. And again, in the modern story of Griffith's four-part epic **Intolerance** (1916), there appear a predatory pimp, thieves and gunmen (not to mention a dramatic car-chase). But these are only embryonic ancestors of the classic movie hoods of the Thirties, contemporary versions of the cruel landlords and lecherous villains that populated Griffith's more blatantly Victorian melodramas. Only with the release of **Underworld** in 1927 did a more recognizably modern urban criminal appear on screen.

Written by Ben Hecht, formerly a Chicago crime-reporter, **Underworld** has as its central characters burly thief Bull Weed (George Bancroft), his girl Feathers (Evelyn Brent) and his drunken lawyer pal Rolls Royce (Clive Brook). As directed by Josef Von Sternberg – the man who would later achieve enormous success with his films starring Marlene Dietrich – the story focuses less on crime itself than on a tangled love triangle. Even Bull is barely a fully-fledged gangster; he specializes in robbing banks and jewelry stores, while bootlegging and racketeering are hardly mentioned. And yet many of the film's scenes and images were immensely influential on later pictures: the flighty moll, a gangsters' ball, a flower-shop killing, a final epic shoot-out with the cops, all taking place within a city shrouded in apparently almost perpetual night.

The seeds of the gangster film had been sown; with the arrival of the talkies following soon after – a development that would allow audiences to hear the screaming of sirens, the firing of guns, the revving of cars, and the slick nasal slang of the heroes – the seeds would grow into a robust and shady tree of huge proportions.

The seminal status of **Little Caesar** lies in the way it

Below left: Massara and moll prepare to meet their doom: Douglas Fairbanks Jr played the sidekick of **Little Caesar** whose love for his partner in a cabaret-dancing job drives Rico into a jealous rage.

Below: James Cagney in his second movie role, in **Doorway to Hell** (1930). The film was advertised by Warner Brothers as "the life story of Lou 'Legs' Ricarno", to cash in on the notoriety of Legs Diamond, then much in the news.

Bottom: An archetypal mobster-movie scene. Though **Doorway to Hell** was hardly a great gangster film – mainly because of the use of suave Lew Ayres as Legs Ricarno – it did set a few fashions in the use of tommy-guns and fast black limos.

Underworld (1927).
Right: Josef Von Sternberg's baroque gangland romance may look dated these days, but upon release it seemed "powerful... realistic... absorbing", and had queues stretching around the block. Behind bars is George Bancroft as the prototypical hoodlum Bull Weed.

Below: The end of a hard night on the town at a gangsters' ball. Looking understandably annoyed with her drunken partner is Evelyn Brent who, as Feathers, became one of Sternberg's first femme fatales.

established the ritualistic rise-and-fall storyline and the recurring symbols of the classic gangster movie: time and again, the films revolve around seedy speakeasies and opulent nightclubs, ostentatious clothes and penthouse apartments, dark and empty backstreets, flashing guns, fast limos, flighty dames, and gangs of dumb thugs paying court to their proud leader. It also set the formula for the typical mobster hero: a Catholic immigrant (Italian or Irish) rising from the gutters, ruthlessly using and exterminating all around him (including friends and partners, frequently described as too soft); vain, conceited, respectful of success but contemptuous of respectability, and— more often than not—sexually abnormal (Rico is a manic woman-hater, and possibly also a repressed homosexual in his jealousy towards Joe Massara's involvement with a night-club dancer).

Echoes of Little Caesar

Of the dozens of gangster movies produced each year by Hollywood during the early Thirties, many are now lost, and many more are unremarkable, repetitively churning out the formulas that had proved so attractive in **Little Caesar**. Of the more notable examples, **Doorway to Hell*** (1930) lacked the hard, steely quality of the Robinson film, with Lew Ayres portraying a gentleman vagabond rather than a hoodlum; Von Sternberg's **Thunderbolt** (1929) again starred the rather wooden George Bancroft (who was Bull Weed in **Underworld**) in a slow-moving tale of doubt, distrust and betrayal set largely in a prison; and master-stylist Rouben Mamoulian's **City Streets** (1931), starring Gary Cooper and Sylvia Sidney, remains

first and foremost a love-story, despite taking place in the world of bootleggers and mob rule—it even manages not to show a single killing on screen. The next great gangster classic, in fact, was William Wellman's **The Public Enemy*** (1931), notable mainly for introducing James Cagney to cinema audiences.

The film's action starts in 1909, with the importance of alcohol firmly established in the opening shots of breweries, beer-carts, and bars. Street-urchins Tom Powers (Cagney) and Matt Doyle (Edward Woods) are already on the road to ruin, indulging in petty theft and generally mischievous behavior. By the time Prohibition arrives in 1920, they have already graduated to more serious crime, having broken into a furrier's and killed a policeman. Now cockily confident, money-hungry, and violent, Tom and Matt take their places in a city bootlegging mob and indulge in battles against rival gangs until they both meet violent ends.

Cagney's power

The Public Enemy not only lays more stress on bootlegging as *the* criminal activity of the Twenties than did **Little Caesar**; it also attempts to fill in the social backgrounds to the boys' criminal ways more clearly. But no effort is made, even in the childhood prologue, to explain why the pair are destined for the criminal life, while the portrait of Tom Powers' family is embarrassingly sentimentalized: his "good" brother (Donald Cook) comes across as a self-righteous prig, while the kindly, doting mother (Beryl Mercer) now seems like a simpering moron who understands nothing at all about either her children

Left: Reflections in a bootlegger's eye. The Kid (Gary Cooper) and Nan Cooley (Sylvia Sidney) find love in a hall of mirrors, in Rouben Mamoulian's **City Streets** (1931), a gangland saga that doesn't show a single death on screen.

Below: Barely a fully-fledged mobster, George Bancroft's Bull Weed in **Underworld** was rather an unusually violent version of the gentleman jewel thief. Here he brandishes his tommy-gun as the police close in on his hideout.

The Public Enemy (1931).
Left: The end of the road for Matt Doyle (Edward Woods), the man originally intended to take the lead part. After director William Wellman realized the energetic James Cagney's superior acting talents, Woods became mere sidekick to Cagney's Tom Powers.

Right: The hard sell. Tom Powers (James Cagney) tries out new and agressive sales tactics on a barman who is reluctant to buy his bootleg booze. (**The Public Enemy** was the first major gangster film to stress bootlegging as the basis of gangland economy.)

Far right: The inimitably fierce and contemptuous sneer of James Cagney who, though he rarely played gangsters, became fixed in audiences' minds as *the* archetypal hood.

Below right: Brutal brotherly love. Tony Camonte (Paul Muni) yields to his feelings of jealousy towards his sister Cesca (Ann Dvorak) in the 1932 version of **Scarface**.

or the ways of the world. But **The Public Enemy** is first and foremost Cagney's film, and the power of his first starring performance is indeed memorable.

There is an immoral charisma to Cagney's performance both in life – where he is dynamically energetic, manically quick-tempered and violent, and given to brutish acts such as pushing a grapefruit into his mistress' face and shooting a horse that has fatally thrown a friend – and in death – being trussed up by rivals in blankets, bandages and ropes, and dumped on Ma's doorstep like some obscene mummy. This charisma transcends those unfortunate scenes when, untypically, he apologizes to his family for his evil ways. His success in the role led to his being forever considered as *the* archetypal screen gangster, even though during the golden years of the early Thirties he rarely played a gangster as such.

The sentimentality that mars **The Public Enemy** and the uncharacteristic repentance shown by Tom Powers towards the end of the film robs him of Rico Bandello's perverse dignity. Far more artistically successful and less morally compromised was Howard Hawks' brilliant **Scarface** (1932), starring Paul Muni as Tony Camonte, a thoroughly warped and heartless hoodlum who unaccidentally has the same nickname as Al Capone. **Scarface** is the familiar tale of a gun-crazy punk on the up-and-up who meets a savagely violent end, and could easily have been just another gangster movie. But writer Ben Hecht and director Hawks sprinkled the basic material with unusual and effectively perverse ideas, the result being the finest of all early mobster pictures.

An important element was Hawks' decision to fashion the conception of Camonte and his sister Cesca (Ann Dvorak) after the decadence of the Borgias, so that the gangster's absurd

possessiveness and protectiveness toward her is rooted in incestuous desire. It is this desire, in fact, that leads to his final demise: outraged and insanely jealous when he discovers that Cesca has become the lover of his best friend Rinaldo (George Raft), he shoots his partner and thus suffers *both* remorse and confusion *and* the burning hatred of his beloved sister. The emotional turmoil leads him to make uncharacteristic errors just as the cops finally close in on him.

"X" for death
Equally perverse and macabre elements course throughout the film. Each time one of Camonte's rivals is killed, an "X" appears somewhere in the visual composition – for example, when gangleader Gaffney (Boris Karloff) is murdered at a bowling alley, he has just marked his score card with an "X" for a strike. This witty touch evokes not only the traditional Christian crucifix but also the cross used in "rubbing out" or erasing an error in writing. Much black humor is also had at the expense of Tony's moronic secretary, who can never understand how telephones work and even attempts to shoot one when the speaker at the other end of the line insults him. But Camonte is the character who is most memorably amoral: brutishly stupid (he interprets the writ of Habeas Corpus as "dey gotta have der body") yet sharply streetwise in his murderous strategies, callously charming and treacherous in his pursuit of his boss's girlfriend (Karen Morley), totally selfish (not least in the treatment of his adored Cesca) and ruthlessly ambitious. Even his one apparently "cultural" quality – a love of opera – is given a darkly ironic twist by the fact that he has a penchant for whistling an aria from *Lucia di Lammermoor* before shooting his victims.

Scarface stretched the conventions of the gangster movie to

their limits. It is darker, faster, more violent and immoral than any other film of the period. A work of astounding virtuosity from its opening moments when an unseen assassin shoots a gangleader who has just advised his friends "A man's always gotta know when he's got enough", to the irony of the hero's final death in the gutter beneath a Thomas Cook's sign stating "The World Is Yours", the film retains the power to shock and excite over fifty years after it was made. It is perhaps appropriate that such an amoral film, which challenged the Hays Code in such an invigorating fashion, should come at the end of the first classic gangster cycle. **Scarface** had gone as far in its depiction of violence and brutality as the gangster film could at that time go.

Mobster movies did of course continue after **Scarface** but by and large they were tired affairs, relying on the safe, tame regurgitation of old material. Increasingly, self-parody became fashionable, with Edward G. Robinson displaying his comic talents in films like **The Little Giant** (1933), **The Whole Town's Talking** (1935), **A Slight Case of Murder** (1938), and Cagney turning in a very funny performance in **Lady Killer** (1933) in which he plays a gangster on the run who hides out in Hollywood and, by crooked means, becomes a heart-throb film star. At the same time, under pressure from the Hays Code and groups like the Catholic Legion of Decency, not to mention the FBI, who all objected to Hollywood's glorification of criminals, stars like Cagney and Robinson were now to be found fighting on the right side of the law in movies like **G-Men** (1935) and **Bullets or Ballots** (1936). After Franklin Roosevelt abolished Prohibition on December 5th, 1933, gangsters could no longer be looked on in the same unquestioning heroic light as before.

Last of a dying breed

It is hardly surprising then that when the second cycle of gangster movies started up in the late Thirties, they were accompanied by a new set of values inherited from serious drama and prevailing political thought. A new, strained and semi-philosophical seriousness was introduced in a handful of movies adapted from Broadway theatrical hits. Film versions of Robert E. Sherwood's **The Petrified Forest** and Maxwell Anderson's **Winterset** were released in 1936, and of Sidney Kingsley's **Dead End** in 1937. All treated the gangster as if he were the last tragic member of a dying breed: the man of action, successor to the frontiersman of the Old West. These films now look dreary, over-inflated and pretentious, rendered leaden by static action and inappropriately pseudo-poetic dialogue. Only the presence of Humphrey Bogart, in fact, gives a spark of cinematic life to **The Petrified Forest** and **Dead End**.

Sherwood's play, for example, places gangster-on-the-run Duke Mantee (Bogart) in a claustrophobic confrontation with pontificating poet Leslie Howard, a confrontation that results in a grudging and totally artificial acknowledgment that both characters are obsolete dinosaurs in a Brave New World personified by dreamy waitress Bette Davis.

Amidst all the high-falutin' sentiments, Bogart's taciturn performance blows like a breath of fresh air; barely responsive to the poet's claim that he, Mantee, is a fine but outdated example of rugged individualism and violence, Bogart expresses all that needs to be said with a series of sneering, snarling monosyllables before shooting the poet and attempting to escape from the heavily theatrical atmosphere of the roadside diner.

Fortunately, in comparison with these stagy and unconvincing movies, the new social conscience that permeated Hollywood during the Roosevelt years was a lively and none too serious affair. Although it was now fashionable to locate the roots of criminal behavior in poverty, injustice, prejudice and the like,

Scarface (1932).
Above: "The South Side ain't big enough for the both of us!" Tony Camonte (Paul Muni) decides to get tough with boss Johnny Lovo (Osgood Perkins, left). Lovo's girl Poppy (Karen Morley) and Tony's sidekick Rinaldo (George Raft) look on.

Above right: Tony Camonte's methods of dealing with business competitors yield bloody results. In fact **Scarface** was deemed so violent that its makers were forced to subtitle it **The Shame of a Nation**.

Lady Killer (1933).
Left: James Cagney as mobster Dan Quigley, in a comedy thriller cleverly constructed around film-goers' perceptions of the star's image. Quigley, on the run, hides out in Hollywood and becomes a star.

Far left: Hoodlum in Hollywood. Although **Lady Killer** made great and effective use of Cagney's much underrated comic talents, it also had its fair share of violent thrills, playing upon his image of a wild urban animal.

Below: George Bancroft and director Josef Von Sternberg attempted to recreate the excitement of **Underworld** in **Thunderbolt** (1933). Sadly the film – set largely in a prison – was too slow and verbose to match up to the earlier film.

Hollywood's philistine and commercial practices never allowed sermonizing to overshadow the audience's desire for action.

A new deal, a new conscience

In some films, the simplistic sociological angle was dressed up with exemplary intelligence. Fritz Lang's **You Only Live Once** (1937), for example, one of the earliest rural gangster pictures very loosely inspired by the exploits of Bonnie and Clyde, cast Henry Fonda as a small-time thief who tries to go straight after being released from prison. But people on the outside are so narrow-minded in their condemnation of anyone with a criminal record that he not only finds it hard to get work and lodgings but is also blamed for an armed robbery he did not commit. Embittered, suspicious of the legal system, and desperate, he ends up resorting to criminal violence before finally being shot down by the Law.

Lang's film was unusually bleak in comparison to most social-conscience crime films coming out of Hollywood, largely because the web of circumstance and Fate woven around Fonda's predicament is so tight and inescapable. Not surprisingly, Warner Brothers – who had introduced the gangster movies with **Little Caesar** and **The Public Enemy** – contributed lighter examples to the genre. Cagney, for example, appeared in an effective slice of conscience-stirring, Michael Curtiz's **Angels with Dirty Faces** (1938), where his local hero gangster Rocky is viewed as a product of the Lower East Side slums. The only reason his old friend Father Jerry Connolly (Pat

O'Brien) didn't take the same criminal route through life is that, when as boys they were involved in a street crime together, Rocky was caught and became an habitual criminal after his prison stretch, whereas Jerry got away and saw the light.

The focus of the film, however, is not so much on crime – Cagney wants to take his revenge on shyster partner Bogart who has tricked him out of a fortune – but on the souls of the kids who populate the slums and worship Cagney's every misdemeanor. The guttersnipes admire his courage and want to follow his example; and the film centers on whether Father Jerry can persuade Rocky to make them despise him. Rocky resists, but when caught and sentenced to death for killing Bogart, in an ending both ludicrous and moving he yields to the good priest's persuasion and lets out a cowardly scream as he's led to the electric chair. The kids, disappointed by their hero's suddenly turning yellow, are presumably saved.

In spite of attempting to explain crime as an environmental disease, **Angels with Dirty Faces** finally treats the subject as a conflict between heroic individuals: Rocky and Jerry battling for the souls of innocents. Again in **Each Dawn I Die** (1939) in which Cagney finds himself jailed for a crime he did not commit, fighting against corrupt politicians and finding true friendship with habitual yet honorable hoodlum George Raft, the social comment is muted by the cult of the power of personality. More realistic, however, is Raoul Walsh's **The Roaring Twenties** (1939), a fast-moving compendium of gangster-movie conventions embellished with a sense of social change.

Far left: Danger in the desert. Diner waitress Bette Davis and philosopher-poet Leslie Howard are threatened by surly gangster on the run Humphrey Bogart. The young Bogie's snarling performance as Duke Mantee was by far the best thing in the stagey **The Petrified Forest** (1936).

Bogart's tough, craggy appearance *(above)* and lisping snarl brought him plenty of opportunities to play the hoodlum in the films of the late Thirties. Here *(left)* he sports a natty jacket and a threatening manner in William Wyler's adaptation of **Dead End** (1937).

Top: Trapped by the Law. Young and innocent Eddie Taylor (Henry Fonda) gets a bum rap after being imprisoned for an armed bank robbery he did not commit, in Fritz Lang's **You Only Live Once** (1937), one of the bleakest gangster movies of the decade.

The Roaring Twenties

The film begins with Eddie Bartlett (Cagney) and George Hally (Bogart) meeting up in the trenches of the First World War while American soldiers are struggling "to make the world safe for democracy". Immediately it is clear that Eddie is a regular guy, while George, trigger-happy and given to killing off 15-year-old Huns with vicious glee, has not an ounce of decent human emotion within him.

Back home after the war Eddie finds that unemployment and Prohibition have settled in with such a vengeance that he can't have his old pre-war job back. So much for returning heroes and democracy. He accidentally gets caught up in the world of bootlegging, and his involvement and success in crime steadily increase, until he is ruined by the Depression and eventually forced to fight it out with George (now a thoroughly treacherous and heartless thug) to save the skin of an old war-time buddy, who has become an Assistant District Attorney putting the heat on George's mob. The inevitable heroic death occurs, and Eddie's stoic moll (Gladys George) offers his epitaph: "He used to be a big shot."

The Roaring Twenties, in many ways a determinedly old-fashioned film when made in 1939, nevertheless impresses partly through its relentless pace, partly by the way it suggests that in times of upheaval almost everyone is corruptible. Goodness and evil are presented as relative, not absolute: everyone – even Priscilla Lane, the good girl Cagney comes to love – is tainted and to some extent at home in sordid, illegal speakeasies and bootlegging factories; while everyone, except Bogart, is presented as having some human kindness in them.

This acknowledgement that moral qualities lie on a grayish spectrum rather than being black or white, coupled with the film's inserted documentary episodes stating the importance of events like the start of Prohibition, the Wall Street Crash, and the introduction of Big Business into crime, make for a more complex view of gangsterdom than had been previously portrayed.

Angels with Dirty Faces (1938). *Left:* Across the Great Divide. Convict Rocky (James Cagney) discusses his return to freedom with his crooked partner James Frazier (Bogart).

Bottom left: "Good" gangster Rocky Sullivan has a little disagreement with his treacherous partner-in-crime Frazier.

Bottom center: Rocky Sullivan shows the near-delinquent Dead End Kids how to keep their noses clean.

The Roaring Twenties (1939). *Below:* Danny Green (Frank McHugh), Eddie Bartlett (Cagney) and George Hally (Bogart) — bootleggers with a mission to survive the Depression.

Top left: Tart-with-a-heart Panama (Gladys George) comforts her melancholy baby Eddie Bartlett.

Swansong to an era

The Second World War, however, had now become of greater interest than the criminal war at home, and many of the great real-life gangsters whose names everyone knew were either dead or in prison. The example set by **The Roaring Twenties** would not be followed for many years; the gangster movie was largely absent from the Forties, while the private eye and returning war-veteran took over as heroes in the crime thriller. But the classic gangster film did receive a magnificent swansong in 1941 in the form of Raoul Walsh's **High Sierra**. Loosely inspired by the character of rural gangster John Dillinger, it stars Bogart as Roy Earle, an aging mobster out of prison and planning to perform one last robbery before retiring.

Earle is viewed as a quiet, lonely and honorable man; his sheer professionalism is highlighted by the clumsy talkative youngsters he is given to do the job with. Although there are some faintly embarrassing scenes which stress his essential decency in wanting to help cure a crippled girl he meets, Earle's dignity derives more or less totally from this professionalism and from the quiet wisdom with which he is endowed by age and experience. Social circumstances are of little concern to Walsh here.

What matters is the gangster's epic status, confirmed once and for all by his death in the monumental gray cliffs of the Sierra Nevada, where he is trapped by faceless cops and a sensation-hungry crowd. As played, unsentimentally, by Bogart, Earle's death is a tragedy of Fate; there is no other way out for him. It is a fine and moving ending to the Golden Years of gangster films.

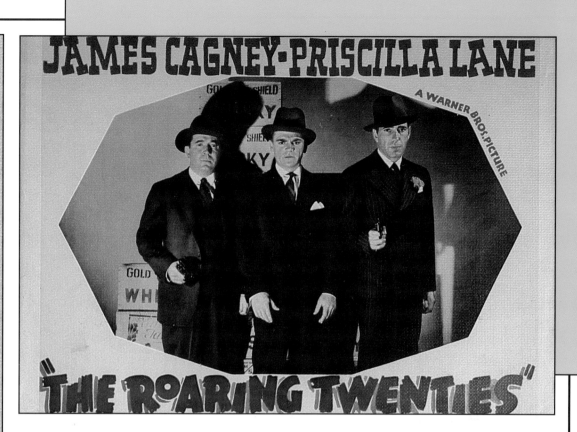

JAMES CAGNEY·PRISCILLA LANE

A WARNER BROS. PICTURE

"THE ROARING TWENTIES"

Left: Before attaining respectability as a detective in **The Maltese Falcon** (1941), Bogart played hoods in many a minor mobster movie. In **King of the Underworld** (1939), he was a gangster finally caught when the gorgeous Ms Francis blinds him.

Above: In retrospect it's strange to see Priscilla Lane getting star-billing with Cagney for **The Roaring Twenties** (1939) – all too sugary as the good girl Cagney falls for, she's far less interesting now than Gladys George's portrayal of the world-weary Panama.

Right: With a life expectancy as short as his haircut, Roy Earle (Bogart) has good reason to look worried, even though devoted moll Marie Garson tries to comfort him. Raoul Walsh's **High Sierra** (1941) was the first, and best, version of W. R. Burnett's classic crime novel.

Left: The last great gangster movie of pre-war Hollywood, **High Sierra** (1941), was also Bogart's last truly great mobster role before he switched to the other side of the law as Sam Spade in **The Maltese Falcon** (1941).

Below: Betrayed by the barking of his faithful mutt Pard, Roy "Mad Dog" Earle (Bogart) meets a tragic death on the cold, gray cliffs of the **High Sierra**. Left behind to mourn him is faithful moll Marie (Ida Lupino).

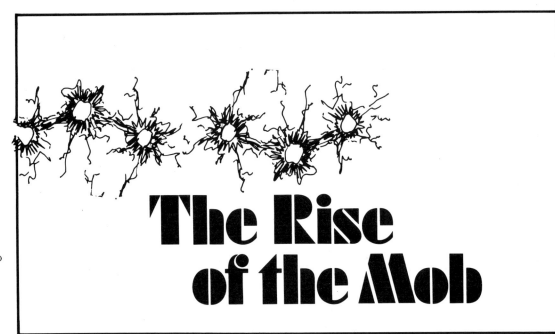

The Rise of the Mob

Bubbles and bullets: Johnny Rocco (Edward G. Robinson) reveals his psychological insecurity by taking his tommy-gun into the bath with him, in John Huston's excellent **Key Largo** (1948).

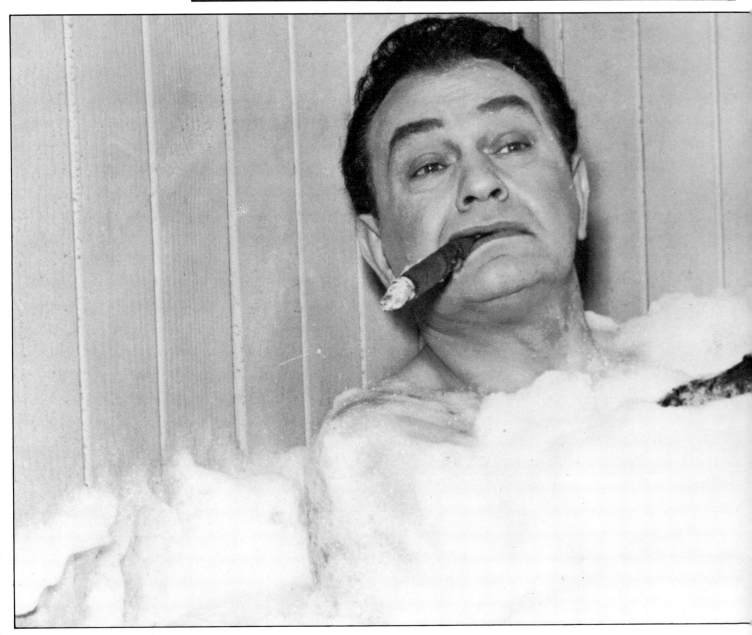

The Second World War greatly damaged America's optimism about the order of things. The holocaust in Europe and Asia had revealed that the world had a shocking capacity for evil and violence, while also opening wide the fissures in an American society itself derived from the Old World and consisting of immigrant communities from a huge variety of nations. And despite victory, the fear of Communism in the post-war years that gave rise to the McCarthy witch-hunts bred distrust, betrayal, and an increasing paranoia about nationwide conspiracies. This all-embracing fear of widespread plotting and corruption could not but be reflected in the movies, both in the explicit "Cold War" films and in the gangster genre; crime was now seen as something far more organized and dangerous than the one-time exploits of individuals like Little Caesar and Scarface.

This is not to say that the old-fashioned gangster-movie did not survive. Edward G. Robinson yet again took up the mantle in John Huston's **Key Largo** (1948) as aging gangleader Johnny Rocco, holding the guests in a Florida hotel hostage while he waits to find a route back into the country (he has been deported). The film in fact bears more resemblance to **Casablanca** (1943) than to **Little Caesar**, since it homes in on

whether cynical and self-centered war-veteran Bogart will finally make a moral choice and take up arms against Rocco and his hoods. But Robinson lends great color to his role, maltreating his drunken moll (Claire Trevor), whispering obscenities into the ear of war-widow Lauren Bacall, and becoming noticeably scared when a storm blows up. The storm acts as a dramatic symbol of Rocco's inner turmoil, revealing the gangster movie's increased concern with psychology.

A case of Freuditis

That interest – America was now suffering from an acute case of Freuditis – was taken even further in Walsh's **White Heat** (1949). James Cagney's Cody Jarrett, a bank-robbing hoodlum of the old school, is a million miles away from his Tom Powers in **The Public Enemy**; whereas Tom was simply a violent youth who'd grown up on the wrong side of the tracks, Cody is a fully-fledged psychopath, suffering from a severe Oedipal complex. Deeply insecure, plagued by migraines, he is thoroughly dependent on his mother (Margaret Wycherly) for guidance and affection; he even at one point sits on her lap – only an actor of Cagney's ability and fire could attempt such a scene without looking ridiculous. His dependence on Ma leads to his downfall; when

Ma is killed by his wife's lover, Cody's judgement is blinded and he turns to undercover Treasury agent Edmond O'Brien as a replacement confidant. The T-men finally trap Cody and his gang during a daring heist, and the demented hoodlum, cornered on top of a gas cylinder, blows himself up: "Top of the world, Ma!" The final image of an uncontrollable conflagration is the perfect symbol of the lethal emotional turmoil in Cody's soul.

Other conventional gangster-movies followed – most notably Cagney again in **Kiss Tomorrow Goodbye** (1950), vicious and energetic as ever. But for the most part, a very different portrait of crime was presented during the Fifties. As early as 1947, **Kiss of Death** had intimated at the existence of an organized mob with wide-ranging powers, when small-time hood Victor Mature finds nowhere to hide from the Outfit's vengeance after he has turned informer. And in **Force of Evil** (1949) crooked lawyer John Garfield is doomed to experience similar problems after he betrays his numbers-racketeering colleagues. But the most interesting aspect of **Force of Evil** is its equation of ruthless criminal activity with big-business; corruption is seen to infect even the hallowed banks of Wall Street. The American Dream has gone rotten.

Tackling organized crime
Still, however, no explicit mention had been made of any criminal organization devoted purely to crime and wielding power beyond the confines of a neighborhood or city. Only with the publication of the findings of the Senate Crime Investigating Committee, chaired by Senator Estes Kefauver in 1950-1, did Hollywood feel ready to deal more openly with the idea of organized crime.

In **The Enforcer*** (1951) Humphrey Bogart plays crusading Assistant District Attorney Ferguson, loosely based on Burton Turkus, the man who a decade earlier had revealed the existence of Murder, Inc., an assassination bureau working under the general control of the National Crime Syndicate and operated by Albert Anastasia and "Lepke" Buchalter. While investigating a murder puzzle, Ferguson discovers the existence of a large and extremely methodical organization that carries out "contracts" on victims, using motiveless gunmen to perform an impersonal "hit". Despite showing murders, the film lays emphasis not so much on violence as on the criminal system and on the enormity of the organization's influence, able to silence potential witnesses through fear and death.

Following the example of **The Enforcer**, gangster films repeatedly portrayed the underworld as consisting of groups of mobsters working together in organizations fascinatingly similar to the majority of capitalist businesses and frequently masking their criminal activities behind an ultra-respectable facade. In 1951 Hollywood produced **The Racket** and **The Mob**, in 1952 **Captive City** and **Hoodlum Empire**, in 1953 **The System** and **The Big Heat**. Most impressive is the last, directed by Fritz Lang and revealing that *nobody*, however outwardly respectable, is beyond corruption and the influence of the Mob.

Gang-boss Mike Lagana (Alexander Scourby) and his extremely violent henchman Vince Stone (Lee Marvin) count amongst their friends not only other hoods but also the Police Commissioner and a City Counselor, both seen fraternizing around poker tables with acknowledged killers. Politics are also corrupt: at one point Lagana tells Stone to avoid publicity and make his killings more discreet because, "the elections are too

Key Largo (1948).
Far left: The gathering storm. Humphrey Bogart faces up to thug-with-a-gun Thomas Gomez watched by Lionel Barrymore and Lauren Bacall.

Overleaf: Lauren Bacall, nursing one of Johnny Rocco's victims, looks to Bogart for help.

White Heat (1949).
Overleaf: Behind bars without women. Mother-fixated Cody Jarrett (Cagney) taunts Hank Fallon (Edmond O'Brien) about his wife's photo.

Left: Up against the wall. After the success of White Heat, Cagney again played an aging gangster in Kiss Tomorrow Goodbye (1950).

Bottom: Cagney beginning to have suspicions about undercover man Fallon.

close. Things are changing in this country. I don't want to end up in the same ditch with the Lucky Lucianos."

Big-time mobsters

Lagana is the power in the city that "kinda runs things. That's no secret." And yet he himself never actually appears to commit a crime; his well-paid thugs do all the dirty work for him, while he consorts with public officials at his large, elegant and eminently respectable mansion. Similar portraits of big-time mobsters and organized crime followed: **The Big Combo** (1955) with Richard Conte as the suave, cool Mr Brown (he has erased all evidence of his Italian origins), so powerful as to make it almost impossible for cop Cornel Wilde to gather evidence against him; **On the Waterfront** (1954), an acknowledgement of the Mob's involvement in dockside labor racketeering, with Johnny Friendly (Lee J. Cobb) exercising total and corrupt power over a huge workforce of ordinary men; **The Phenix City Story** (1955), a semi-documentary re-creation of crime-busting in a city entirely given to criminal ways, to such an extent that the National Guard had to be called in to restore law and order; **The Garment Jungle** (1957) about corruption in the clothes trade, rife with profiteering and protection rackets; **The Brothers Rico** (1957) in which retired mobster Richard Conte sets out to expose the Syndicate after it has killed his brother, and finds a criminal dragnet out to stop and kill him that is more efficient and geographically more wide-ranging than anything the police can offer; and, most impressively, Sam Fuller's **Underworld USA** (1961) which views its villains as a hierarchy of ruthless businessmen operating from a deceptively normal skyscraper under the corporate name of National Projects.

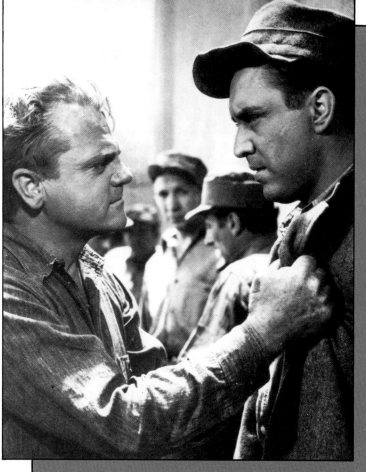

Working in modern streamlined offices almost identical to those of the FBI – which itself is employing a vengeful criminal (Cliff Robertson) to destroy the Mob – the gangleaders all head separate departments of the conglomerate: Narcotics, Prostitution, Gambling. Yet National Projects also has its own swimming pool which it regularly opens up to deprived children. The Syndicate, on the outside at least, appears to be indistinguishable from any other large-scale business concern. And it is money, not the power and respect that Rico Bandello so desired, that is the *raison d'être* of criminal activity. Crime now *is* business.

Although throughout the decade's Syndicate movies the emphasis had been on corruption and organization rather than violence, that is not to say that violence did not occur. And when it was portrayed, as if to compensate for the criminals' outward respectability, it was more baroque, perverse and callously impersonal than ever before. In **The Big Heat**, for example, mention is made of torture by cigarette burns, and Lee Marvin and Gloria Grahame toss pots of boiling coffee into each other's faces. In **The Big Combo**, Richard Conte tortures the cop by fitting him with the hearing-aid of his elderly, hard-of-hearing henchman (Brian Donlevy) and turning up a radio to ear-splitting volume. Rod Steiger in **On the Waterfront** betrays the Mob and is rewarded by being suspended half-way up a wall on a vicious longshoreman's hook. And in **Underworld USA** the cool, calm, and good-looking assassin hired by National Projects ruthlessly runs down the young daughter of an informer, even though he admits to enjoying helping out at the Swim Meets for underprivileged kids. Cruel, cold killing, a long way indeed from the fiery and personal tommy-gun slayings of the early Thirties.

Keeping hoodlums off the screen

The impersonality and business-orientation of the Syndicate movies was, however, counterbalanced by more fiercely individualistic movies celebrating the deeds of famous gangsters then dead or in prison. At the time of John Dillinger's death in 1934, the Hays Code had laid down censorship restrictions banning any efforts to portray real-life hoodlums on the screen. Names like Dillinger, Bonnie and Clyde, Baby Face Nelson, and Ma Barker – all rural desperadoes – and city hoods like Al Capone, Hymie Weiss and Dutch Schultz had therefore been either ignored or turned into vaguely similar fictional figures. Ma Barker (in **Machine Gun Mama**) and **Roger Touhy, Gangster*** had both been dealt with explicitly in 1944, but only in very minor low-budget productions; the first biography of a really big-name hood came the following year. Made for Poverty Row's Monogram Pictures by the King Brothers – themselves former bootleggers working on the margins of the film industry – **Dillinger** became the surprise hit of 1945.

It is perhaps hard now to see why such a tacky low-budget film should have done so well at the box-office; perhaps audiences were just keen to see *any* film account of one of the Thirties' most notorious criminals. A dour, unglamorous affair, the film strays wildly from the known facts (anyway, it is still not certain that Dillinger himself actually killed anyone during his brief stint of bank-robbing). Melvin Purvis, the G-Man who finally tracked down a man claimed to be Dillinger and had him shot outside a Chicago cinema – where he'd seen **Manhattan Melodrama**, a glossily unrealistic 1934 gangster vehicle from MGM starring Clark Gable – is never mentioned in the film, while it turns the real-life Lady in Red – a Rumanian immigrant threatened with deportation who hoped for FBI help if she betrayed Dillinger – into a far less interesting and more conventional moll.

Nevertheless, for all its weaknesses, the film still exerts some fascination; much of it consists of old stock footage of car-chases, robberies and gunfights (including the celebrated bank-robbery scene from **You Only Live Once**), strung together with scant regard for continuity or characterization. The result is a very fast, immoral film of strange stylistic simplicity – a quality enhanced by Lawrence Tierney's unsympathetic performance.

Kiss of Death (1947).
Far left: Having informed on his criminal colleagues, Victor Mature looks understandably worried.

Bottom left: Richard Widmark (with Victor Mature). His performance as the sadistic gunman Tommy Udo was so strong that he was typecast as a psychotic for some time afterwards.

Left: Small time racketeer Thomas Gomez is punished by Syndicate thugs in **Force of Evil** (1949).

Below: Detective Robert Mitchum gets his man. Mobster Robert Ryan, head of **The Racket** (1952), is able to evade the long arm of the law no more.

Mitchum and Ryan were perhaps the two most popular stars under contract to Howard Hughes' RKO studios and appeared in many crime films.

Bottom: **The Captive City** (1952), just one of many movies made in the early Fifties about a small town corrupted by the Mob and cleaned up by a crusading hero (John Forsythe, center) who risks life and limb.

Love and death

Despite the film's financial success, the Hays Code effectively prevented any more gangster-biographies appearing until 1957. But a fashion had been set in movies dealing with rural gangsters – WASP desperadoes reacting to the hardships of the Depression in the South- and Mid-West by turning to bank robbery and kidnapping, rather than city immigrants to bootlegging and organized crime. Most notable were Nicholas Ray's **They Live By Night** (1949) and Joseph H. Lewis' **Gun Crazy** (1950).

Both are fugitive thrillers very loosely inspired by the exploits of Bonnie and Clyde (though taken from pulp novels); but they treat their heroic couples differently. Ray's movie tells of a young member of a bank-robbing gang and his girlfriend. Although living as criminals, Bowie (Farley Granger) and Keechie (Cathy O'Donnell) are presented by Ray as naive, gentle young innocents forced by an unsympathetic world (poverty, unhappy families, prejudice and the pressures of the other gang-members) into an inescapable life of habitual crime. The film indicts society around them as equally corrupt, and the director treats his ill-starred couple to the same touching compassion he would extend to the disaffected young in his later **Rebel Without a Cause** (1955).

Less sentimental and more remarkable is **Gun Crazy**, endowed with a perversity that Lewis repeated in **The Big Combo** five years later. Bart (John Dall) and Laurie (Peggy Cummins) are a far more murderous and amoral couple than Ray's innocents, and yet Lewis engages our sympathies for them, not by making excuses about society, but by emphasizing the depth and loyalty of the passion they feel for one another.

The relentless pacing makes the action so fast that their headlong rush towards crime and death seems inevitable; and yet now and then the film slows down temporarily for moments of tenderness between the pair – tenderness charged with an eroticism rarely depicted in movies of the period. The couple meet at a fairground and are immediately drawn together by their shared interest in guns; gunplay becomes foreplay, with the sexual symbolism made explicit by the openly inviting mutual glances between the two. Later in the film, when they are wanted for a deadly armed robbery, they decide to split up for safety's sake, but can't.

Killers they may be, but their love forces them to risk death rather than to endure separation. Fast, non-moralistic and yet invested with a surprising amount of visual poetry (especially in the final scene when the couple meet death in a misty swamp), **Gun Crazy** is one of the genre's masterpieces, anticipating the movies of the Sixties and Seventies with its investigation of the bonds between sex, money and violence.

Rise of the biopic

Rural gangster pictures continued – including a surprisingly adequate remake of **High Sierra** called **I Died a Thousand Times** (1955) with Jack Palance exceeding all expectations in taking over Bogart's role as Roy Earle – but the next great example of the genre was **Baby Face Nelson** (1957). With Mickey Rooney in fine vicious form as the diminutive hoodlum with a heart of stone, the film charts his criminal life from an attempt to go straight upon leaving prison, to involvement with the Dillinger gang, to his final death at the hands of the FBI. The re-creation of the period – the early Thirties – is perfunctory, with only the cars truly distinguishing the setting from the year in which it was made.

What is interesting, however, is director Don Siegel's conception of Nelson: although a prologue describes him as

TORRID, STARTLING SECRETS OF THE SYNDICATE!

Cornel WILDE
Richard CONTE
Brian DONLEVY
Jean WALLACE IN

THE BIG COMBO

The BIG COMBINATION of Passion, Greed, and Violence That Scorches and Explodes!

Written by PHILIP YORDAN
Produced by SIDNEY HARMON · Directed by JOSEPH LEWIS

AN ALLIED ARTISTS PRODUCTION
Distributed by ASSOCIATED BRITISH-PATHE
Length 7342 ft.   Cert. "A"

THE PHENIX CITY STORY "X"
JOHN McINTIRE · RICHARD KILEY
KATHRYN GRANT
AN ALLIED ARTISTS PRODUCTION
DISTRIBUTED BY ASSOCIATED BRITISH-PATHE LTD.

Above: Kerwin Matthews drags shapely Gia Scala through **The Garment Jungle** (1957).

The Big Heat (1953).
Top left: Case wrapped up. Sergeant Dave Bannion (Glenn Ford) completes his mission of vengeance by arresting Vince Stone (Lee Marvin).

Inset: Debby Marsh (Gloria Grahame) reveals the effect of boiling coffee thrown on a pretty face to Vince Stone.

The Big Combo (1955).
Above center: Cheap it may have been, but Joseph H. Lewis' film was one of the most perverse and original Syndicate movies of the Fifties.

Left: Phil Karlson's semi-documentary style **The Phenix City Story** (1955).

33

Underworld USA (1961).
Left: The shadow of death. The sight that set young Tolly Devlin on the road to a lifetime of delinquency – the murder of his defenseless father by four hoodlums among the garbage cans of a dark and seedy city street.

Bottom: Death by drowning. A watery grave awaits Syndicate boss Connors (Robert Emhardt), assisted on his way by the ruthless Tolly Devlin (Cliff Robertson). Fuller's film was notable for locating its criminal empire within the airy, respectable skyscrapers belonging to an apparently normal business conglomerate.

Right: Elia Kazan's **On The Waterfront** (1954) depicted the Mob's stranglehold over the longshoreman's union, and in celebrating the switch of Terry Malloy (Brando) from thug to informer, also justified its director's own collaboration with McCarthy during the HUAC anti-communist witchhunts.

COLUMBIA PICTURES presents

MARLON BRANDO
On The Waterfront

one whom society failed, the film goes on to present Nelson's murderous ways as fueled by an intense inner drive. Almost totally devoid of any moral sense, profoundly jealous of any man who comes near his girl Sue (Carolyn Jones), he is prone to bouts of manic, irrational temper.

At one point he nearly shoots two harmless, innocent young boys – they are clearly not about to discover his hiding place, but Nelson is by then almost too paranoid to let them live. Siegel's gangster is no folk-hero, but a neurotic: a view of the criminal character that Siegel would pursue further in **The Lineup** (1958), a study of two cold-hearted hired assassins, one a hardened professional, the other so warped in his erratic behavior that he helps, inadvertently, to bring about their final downfall.

Crazed neurotics
Baby Face Nelson set fashions in several respects: the gangster as crazed neurotic, the use of extensive location-shooting in sunlit countryside rather than the artificial city nights of studio sets, and the biopic itself. Subsequent biographies included **The Bonnie Parker Story** (1958), more factually accurate than the Sixties film in that it shows Bonnie to be married – not to Clyde but to another gang-member; Roger Corman's almost comic **Machine Gun Kelly** (1958) which took a not very violent small-time kidnapper and transformed him into a monstrously stupid thug (Charles Bronson), blighted with a neurotic fear of death and a total inability to face up to his scheming moll (Susan Cabot); and films about **Pretty Boy Floyd** (1960), Dutch Schultz (**Portrait of a Mobster**, 1961), **Mad Dog Coll** (1961), Arnold Rothstein (**King of the Roaring Twenties**, 1961) and others. Al Capone was portrayed (not totally accurately) under the name of Rico Angelo (Lee J. Cobb) in Nicholas Ray's nostalgic **Party Girl** (1958); the similarity between Chicago ganglord Rico and the real-life Capone is made most evident in a dinner-scene where Rico brutally beats up a treacherous thug with a silver billiard-cue.

But, like **They Live By Night**, Ray's film is about the healing power of love, set against the violent, colorful backdrop of Chicago during Prohibition: it concentrates on crooked lawyer Robert Taylor and dancer/moll Cyd Charisse trying to go straight and find peace together in the face of lethal opposition from Rico. A love story it might be, but it never steps back from the threat of violence; one of the most unpleasant moments in the history of gangster movies occurs when Rico pours acid on a Christmas-tree paper bell to illustrate what the liquid could do to Charisse's face.

Capone was treated to an explicit biography (Richard Wilson's **Al Capone**) the following year, with Rod Steiger giving a performance both loud and florid – and incidentaly inaccurate in that unlike the character played by Steiger, Capone had no trace of a thick Italian accent. The film's story was a fairly faithful and sensitive account of the mobster's rise to power from acting as a small-time thug for Johnny Torrio to his arrest for tax evasion, although understandably his long, lingering slide into syphilis-induced madness is ignored. The problem with the film is perhaps that it tries to be too respectable; in many ways more a character study than a real gangster film, it tends to knock the life out of its potentially colorful subject-matter.

Immoral tales
No such accusation could be made against **The Rise and Fall of Legs Diamond** (1960), a fast and vivid re-creation of the classic gangster world that portrays character purely through action. As played by Ray Danton, Diamond is totally selfish energy, rocketed to the top of the criminal heap by a sordid mixture of ruthless opportunism, quick thinking, and driving ambition in terms of sex, money and status. Short on psychological analysis, the film nevertheless makes his rise and fall totally convincing by means of its uncompromisingly unsympathetic picture of the "hero". Unremittingly selfish – he abuses his girl (Karen Steele), he lets his brother Eddie (Warren Oates) die in order that his rivals can't "get to" him by holding Eddie as ransom – his egomania is the cause of his own destruction

when a former mistress, no longer able to bear his callously making use of her, betrays him. The darkest of all gangster biopics made in the Fifties, Budd Boetticher's film is also one of the most impressive.

Darkness and nostalgia also were key elements in the decade's one great gangster comedy, **Some Like It Hot** (1959). Much of this well-beloved farce focuses on the complications that set in when jazz-musicians Joe (Tony Curtis) and Jerry (Jack Lemmon) pursue the affections of Sugar Kane (Marilyn Monroe) while dressed up in drag and working for an all-girl band. But the film also delights in playing fast and furiously with references both to real-life events and characters and to earlier gangster movies.

Joe and Jerry dress as women to hide out from Spats Colombo's gang after witnessing a St Valentine's Day massacre of Colombo's rivals; Spats is played by George Raft, a regular in gangster movies and a real-life pal of Bugsy Siegel's (at one point he asks a young hood, spinning a coin, "Where'd ya learn that cheap trick?" – the unspoken answer being from himself, back in **Scarface**); Pat O'Brien, who so often played opposite Cagney during the Thirties and Forties, reappears as a cop; Spats' mob goes to a Florida crime convention for "Friends of Italian Opera" and during a dinner the gangleader – before being shot from inside a birthday cake – threatens to push a grapefruit into a thug's face. Little Bonaparte is upset about the death of Toothpick Charlie – "they used to be choirboys together". Spats tells the cop that his gang – a remarkably ugly and stupid group of mugs – are his "lawyers, all Harvard men". Coffins contain bootleg alcohol, golf-bags conceal tommy-guns, instrument cases conceal – musical instruments.

Some Like It Hot is a comic evergreen, and anyone conversant with the images, dialogue and traditions of gangster-movies – and that includes most cinemagoers – is sure to find the parody and references in the film hilarious. Disrespectful, light-hearted, gaining laughs from all manner of ghastly murderous deeds, it is possibly the most amoral gangster film of all . . . although what was to follow in the Sixties and Seventies would perhaps challenge that status. With censorship being relaxed more and more, new extremes in violence would become the norm.

Far left: Desperado in dire straits. Lawrence Tierney in a tight spot in **Dillinger** (1945).

Gun Crazy (1950).
Bottom left: Love and death. Bart (John Dall) tries to restrain Laurie (Peggy Cummins) in her passion for killing during a daring robbery.

Left: Trapped at last by the forces of Law and Order, Bart hugs Laurie before killing first her, then himself. **Gun Crazy** was Joseph H. Lewis' masterpiece about the lure of sex, violence, and death.

Below: The road to ruin. Jack Palance and Shelley Winters as Roy "Mad Dog" Earle and Marie Garson in **I Died a Thousand Times** (1955), an effective, if inevitably inferior remake of **High Sierra** (1941).

Baby Face Nelson.

Above: Mickey Rooney finds an appropriate place to die in Don Siegel's 1957 masterly film. Rooney's finest performance found strong support from the underrated Carolyn Jones as his faithful moll.

Right: Dangerous double in trouble. Baby Face Nelson (Mickey Rooney) and John Dillinger (Leo Gordon) fight their way out of a tricky situation during a bank-robbery.

Below: The killer as psychotic. Dancer (Eli Wallach) in Don Siegel's **The Lineup** (1958) is just one of the director's many portraits of the mentally unstable man of violence, who brings destruction to himself as well as to others.

Left: An early but extremely effective role for a young Charles Bronson as **Machine Gun Kelly** (1958). Roger Corman's film was so relentless in its depiction of Kelly as a paranoid moron that the film virtually became a black comedy.

Below: Young love caught in a world of greed and corruption. Bowie (Farley Granger) and Keechie (Cathy O'Donnell) are trapped in a nightmarish life of crime, in Nicholas Ray's first feature film **They Live By Night** (1949).

Bottom: Crippled lawyer Tommy Farrell (Robert Taylor) lends a helping hand to gang boss Rico Angelo (Lee J. Cobb) in Nicholas Ray's **Party Girl** (1958). The character of Angelo was loosely based on crime supremo Al Capone.

Left: The St. Valentine's Day Massacre according to Richard Wilson's **Al Capone** (1959). The infamous slaughter of 1929, in which Capone had seven of Bugs Moran's gang killed, is so well documented that any film must portray it faithfully.

Right: Body in the bathroom. Before **Psycho**, Vicki Gaye (Cyd Charisse) discovered her own nightmare behind the shower curtain in **Party Girl**. Lame lover Tommy Farrell (Robert Taylor) joins her in inspecting the work done by his former employers, the Mob.

Below: Dishing out the violence. Legs Diamond (Ray Danton) disturbs a colleague's dinner in Budd Boetticher's **The Rise and Fall of Legs Diamond** (1960), one of the most impressive of all gangster biographies on film. Raw energy, rather than historical accuracy, is the movie's greatest strength, thanks partly to Danton's fiery performance.

Three views of Billy Wilder's
Some Like It Hot (1959).
Far left: Birthday surprise! The
surprise however is that the
recipient of the gift – mobster Spats
Colombo – isn't even celebrating
his birthday! Just one of many
gangster-film clichés turned to
comic effect.

Left: Besotted with Sugar Kane
(Marilyn Monroe), Joe (Tony
Curtis) is unable to emerge from his
disguise as a dame, lest the Mob
discover that he is the man who
witnessed the St. Valentine's
Day Massacre.

Below: Jerry (Jack Lemmon,
second from left) finds it hard to
keep up his pretence that he is a
bona-fide member of an all-girl
traveling jazz band. Singer Sugar
Kane (Monroe, second from right)
helps contribute to the agony and
the ecstasy.

Martyr to the Mafia. Sonny Corleone (James Caan) finds death on the sidewalk after crossing a rival gang in **The Godfather** (1972). Coppola's film glorified the Corleone clan; accordingly the manic Sonny is gunned down while driving to help his sister, rather than during outright gang war.

Rebels and Loners

For no apparent reason – perhaps Hollywood felt unable to compete with television's long-running series *The Untouchables*, which portrayed the ongoing crime-busting activities of Elliot Ness – gangster movies were seldom made for the cinema during the early Sixties. Indeed, before **Point Blank** and **Bonnie and Clyde** arrived in 1967, the most impressive example of the genre was Don Siegel's **The Killers** (1964), which was originally intended for television. A cold, concise thriller distantly inspired by Ernest Hemingway's short story but bearing a close resemblance in plot to an earlier version made by Robert Siodmak in 1946, Siegel's film takes the idea of hoodlums as outwardly respectable citizens to its logical conclusion.

Charlie (Lee Marvin) and Lee (Clu Gulager) are hired assassins of an exceptionally violent nature; the film opens with them barging into a home for the blind, heartlessly threatening the blind receptionist, and casually carrying out their "contract" by pouring bullets into instructor Johnny North (John Cassavetes). And yet these thugs dress like any other smart, middle-class businessmen in trim light-blue suits; Charlie even carries the guns in a brief-case. Having killed North, they set out to discover who hired them and why, a search that leads them to the man who betrayed a gang of bullion-robbers, a paragon of respectability played by Ronald Reagan.

The hoods in **The Killers** have no need of the traditional shadowy back-streets of earlier gangster movies. They are so cool, professional and menacing that they operate without fear in the sunlit suburbs of everyday America.

Cinema vs television

Though made for television, Siegel's tight, taut movie was deemed too violent for the small screen and given a cinema release. It was in fact the changes in censorship, allowing more explicit depiction of sex and violence, that differentiated the modern gangster movie from the pre-1960 model. Violence in particular would become increasingly a factor used by Hollywood to draw audiences away from the television screen and back to the cinemas. Otherwise, in terms of subject matter, the gangster movie barely differed from its Fifties counterpart, dealing either with rural gangsters, the urban syndicate, or the lone desperado intent on preserving his sense of self-respect and independence.

The film that brought the traditional tale of the lone gangster firmly up to date was John Boorman's **Point Blank**. On the

Bonnie and Clyde (1967).
Left: The role that shot Faye
Dunaway to stardom as Bonnie
Parker in **Bonnie and Clyde**
(1967); the late Sixties was a period
of protest and rebellion against
conformism, and the bank-robbing
couple were appropriately
glamorized in Arthur Penn's film.

Inset: Dorothy Provine was
similarly smartened up, if remaining
more of a ruthless character, in an
earlier incarnation of Parker in the
1958 film, **The Bonnie Parker
Story**.

This page: The real-life Bonnie
Parker and Clyde Barrow. Less
physically attractive than Dunaway
and Beatty, they nevertheless
became legends in their own
lifetimes, thanks partly to their
own desire for publicity.

surface, it simply tells of one man's quest for vengeance after a henchman of the Mob has robbed him of money and wife during a crooked cash-transaction in the deserted prison of Alcatraz. But the film is strikingly modern in several respects. On one level, it is an explicit elegy for the passing of old-fashioned individualistic gangsterdom, a cry of despair at the rising power of faceless corporate America: Walker (Lee Marvin) at least acts out of personal feelings of having been betrayed, whereas the Mob – trading as Multiplex – operates purely for money and power. On another level, the film demonstrates the absurdity of the modern world as exemplified by the large-scale capitalism of the Mob: when Walker finally gets to a top man, Brewster (Carroll O'Connor), he is informed that nobody in the Mob actually knows who runs things, and that Brewster cannot give him the cash he wants: "We deal in millions, we never see cash. I got about $11 in my pocket."

This sense of absurdity and pointlessness is extended to Walker's desire for revenge. The final images imply that his quest to eliminate the Mob has never actually taken place, but exists only as a dying man's dream; shot and left to die by a treacherous friend (John Vernon) and a faithless wife (Sharon Acker), Walker fantasizes during his last moments that he can restore his dignity and self-respect by destroying those who have dared to trick him.

Mafia vengeance

Although the fragmented narrative and ironic emphasis on absurdity make **Point Blank** the most self-consciously modernist and "arty" of gangster films, isolating it from more conventional genre-pictures, it was highly influential in its elegiac celebration of an aging loner fighting to preserve his independence in a world of organized corporate crime. **Charley Varrick** (1973) is a small-time hoodlum (Walter Matthau) who is threatened by the Mafia when he inadvertently robs one of their banks; the honor that marks Varrick derives partly from his desire for compensation for the killing of his wife in the course of the robbery, partly because he is the underdog battling against overwhelming odds.

Similarly, in **The Outfit** (1974), Earl Macklin (Robert Duvall) desires to avenge the death of his brother, slain by Mob killers after the Macklins have hit a bank where Mob money is laundered. The relative lightness of Macklin's crimes becomes apparent when gang-boss Robert Ryan tells him, "You want $250,000 from us . . . that's small aggravation. On a good day we take in that much by noon." Macklin's old-fashioned status is also emphasized. "Hard guy," snarls Ryan. "Think you're Dillinger. Goddamn independent, robbing banks. What kind of operation is that?"

Macklin is not glamorized – he's often brutal, obsessive and

Don Siegel's version of Ernest Hemingway's **The Killers** (1964). *Far left:* Death from on high. Sadistic Lee (Clu Gulager) threatens Sheila Farr (Angie Dickinson) after she has lied to him and Charlie his partner in crime.

Bottom left: Browning (Ronald Reagan in his last film role), the mobster mastermind behind a complex bullion-robbery and a treacherous frame-up, prepares to shoot his way out of a tight spot.

Left: Mr Rough Stuff himself, Lee Marvin, as Charlie, the cool, clever and calculating hired assassin, decides he "ain't got the time" to fool around with Sheila Farr (Angie Dickinson).

The Friends of Eddie Coyle (1973).
Below: The immaculately planned and executed bank-robbery at the start of the film.

Bottom: Robert Mitchum in one of his most rewarding roles playing three-time loser Eddie Coyle.

insensitive, especially towards his girlfriend (Karen Black) – but at least he does his dirty work himself, unlike Ryan who surrounds himself with armed lackeys, yes-men, and Doberman dogs. Ryan's presence in the film – like that of a gallery of fine character-actors (Jane Greer, Elisha Cook Jr, Timothy Carey, Marie Windsor, Emile Meyer) familiar from earlier crime thrillers – places the movie squarely in a long cinematic tradition, and adds to the film's emotional force.

In **Prime Cut** (1972) the sympathy that is usually the preserve of the small-time independent is perversely transferred to a Chicago Syndicate enforcer. Lee Marvin's suited hit-man is depicted as a kindly, shy, and calmly professional man with a strong moral sense, whereas Gene Hackman's Kansas racketeer, who hides his illegal activities of peddling drugs and young girls hi-jacked from a local orphanage behind a cattle-farming front, is the real villain: hypocritical, over-ambitious and just a touch insane, he indulges in the sinister habit of killing opponents and sending them back to Chicago in the form of sausages! Surreal, exciting and bizarre, **Prime Cut** plays witty games with gangster-movie conventions, and becomes a weird and wonderful fairy-tale of good battling against evil for the souls of young children.

Death of an informer

In contrast to this gangster-fantasy was **The Friends of Eddie Coyle** (1973), perhaps the most downbeat and realistic of all aging-loner films. Coyle (Robert Mitchum) is blackmailed by Treasury agent Dave Foley (Richard Jordan) into becoming an informer against many of Boston's underworld hoods. As played by Mitchum, Coyle is one of the most memorable and

sympathetic gangsters in years, an unassuming, home-loving man reluctantly collaborating with the Law because another stretch in jail would destroy his family life.

Professional, world-weary, courageous and imbued with a deep sense of honor, his flawed dignity is contrasted with the reckless young punks he encounters in gun-dealing, the ruthless Foley who cares little for his informant's safety, and another informer, Dillon (Peter Boyle), a truly devious example who takes his friend Eddie to an ice-hockey match, gets him drunk, and shoots him through the head as he sleeps on the drive home. The strong performances are supported by a superbly unglamorous portrait of the Boston underworld, a seedy, treacherous milieu where "friends", once they have served their purpose, are all too dispensable.

Many of these films portray violence with an explicitness unthinkable in movies before the Sixties. The film that more than any other set the fashion in lashings of blood and gore was **Bonnie and Clyde**, an enormously popular and influential biopic of Bonnie Parker and Clyde Barrow, the infamous rural desperadoes of the Thirties. In reality, Parker and Barrow were not only a good deal less glamorous than Faye Dunaway and Warren Beatty, their stylish screen incarnations; they were also cold-hearted killers who rarely gave their 14 victims a chance to defend themselves.

But **Bonnie and Clyde** was less concerned with reality (even though most of the events in the film did take place) than with filtering the pair's brief reign of terror through the anarchic sensibilities of the late Sixties. The movie's couple of bandits are clearly meant to reflect the rebellious anti-authoritarian ideas common in America during the late years of the decade.

Left: Fear and loathing in family life. Robert Aldrich's **The Grissom Gang** (1971) contains a motley crew of morons, perverts, and psychotics whose pastime is kidnapping. The film was a violent but cruelly intelligent remake of James Hadley Chase's **No Orchids for Miss Blandish**, previously filmed in Britain in 1948.

Left inset: Martin Sheen in his first major role as the gun-crazy Kit in Terrence Malick's **Badlands** (1974). The film, which detailed the gratuitous killing spree undertaken by two bored, inarticulate teenagers during the Fifties, also made a star of Sissy Spacek, who played Kit's girlfriend Holly.

Right: Robert Altman's **Thieves Like Us** (1974), an impressive and touching remake of Nicholas Ray's **They Live By Night**. Bowie (Keith Carradine, right) rescues fellow bank-robber Chicamaw (John Schuck) from the State Penitentiary.

Bloody Mama (1970). *Bottom:* Mom with a machine-gun Shelley Winters in raucous form as Ma Barker, the brains behind a vicious family of killers in Roger Corman's response to the romanticism of **Bonnie and Clyde**.

Inset below: Ma Barker bemoans the death of son Lloyd (Robert De Niro).

The villain of the piece is Texas Ranger Frank Hamer (Denver Pyle), the humorless and revenge-crazy official who finally tracks the couple down and has them killed in a brutal, treacherous ambush. The gang members, by contrast, kill only in self-defense, and are presented as ordinary folk who, oppressed by the poverty and conformity of the Depression years, are courageous enough to put their dreams into action. When they meet a family of Okie farmers dispossessed of their property by a bank, they cannily introduce themselves with the simple, sympathy-inducing phrase, "We rob banks." And Clyde expresses his ambitions in much the same terms as Little Caesar did almost 40 years earlier; he wants to "get out of the crowd, to be somebody".

Nostalgia and history

Much of the movie is played for laughs, as anti-establishment black comedy. Light, fast and breezy, accompanied by lively country music, it only confronts the real effects of a violent criminal life in the later scenes, when the body count rises dramatically and the fugitives are subjected to a number of dangerous ambushes. Even at the moment of death, however, Bonnie and Clyde are still heroes rather than villains; riddled by countless bullets in an orgy of blood-letting, they remain martyrs to an unhappy period in American history.

With its nostalgic romanticism, its quick, surprising alternations between anarchic humor and harsh violence, and its vision of gangsters as rebellious folk-heroes, **Bonnie and Clyde** dovetailed perfectly into the mood of the time, and became a fashionable if controversial success. Not surprisingly, it inspired numerous offshoots. Exploitation-movie king Roger Corman, who back in the Fifties had followed the lead of **Baby Face Nelson** with **Machine Gun Kelly** and **I, Mobster** (1958) now took up the towel with **The St Valentine's Day Massacre** (1967) and **Bloody Mama** (1970).

The first, focusing on the Capone gang's running battles with rivals Dion O'Banion, Hymie Weiss and Bugs Moran, is possibly the most factually accurate gangster biopic yet made, populated with characters drawn from real life and trotting out documentary evidence through a spoken narration as it charts the events that led to the notorious extermination of seven Chicago hoodlums in a garage on 14 February 1929.

Relatively cheap it may be, but it makes use of an excellent cast that includes Jason Robards (as Capone), George Segal, Ralph Meeker, Bruce Dern and Jack Nicholson, and reduces romanticism to a minimum in a portrait of gang-warfare that is ruthless, and to some extent fueled by racial tensions between the Italians and the Irish.

The rise and fall of Ma Barker

The same anti-romantic vein runs through **Bloody Mama,** apparently conceived in reaction against the light-hearted glamor of **Bonnie and Clyde**; charting the rise and fall of Ma Barker (Shelley Winters) and her four sons, it never hails them as folk-heroes but presents them as a close-knit, incestuous and hideous travesty of normal family life. One of the brothers introduces a new girlfriend into the gang, and her sexual favors are shared with the other boys; the family rows illuminate the abnormal level of love and hate within the group; Lloyd Barker, played by Robert De Niro, is a drug-crazy moron. And it is not the forces of Law and Order that cause the gang's final breakdown, but the unhealthily isolated, manic and self-destructive quality of the family itself.

Although Corman himself gave up directing shortly after making **Bloody Mama,** he was not totally through with gangster movies, going on to produce both **Big Bad Mama**

(1974), a boisterous reworking of the Barker gang story into a tale of a bank-robbing broad (Angie Dickinson) and her two daughters, and **Capone** (1975), a glossy but uninspired rehash of Corman's earlier film that adds interest only through Ben Gazzara's typically charismatic performance and through the conclusion which actually shows the has-been hoodlum

Dillinger.

Left and insets: Three faces of the real John Dillinger – primed for action, the archetypal mug-shot and his death mask. There is some doubt, however, that the man shot outside a Chicago cinema in 1934 was in fact the public enemy at all. The FBI's killing may have been a mistake, or simply a propaganda exercise. In which case, the real Dillinger just might still be alive!

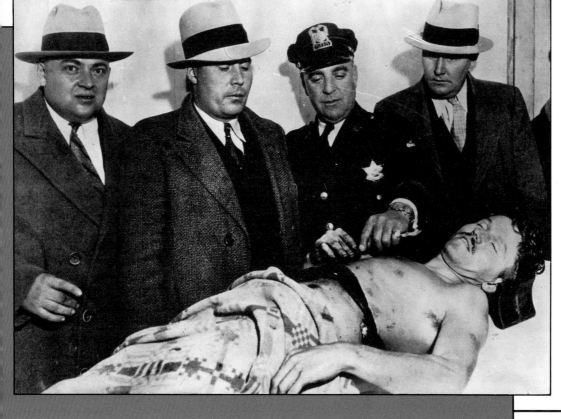

Top left: A fake mug-shot of Lawrence Tierney, playing John Dillinger, in the first screen biography of the gangster in 1945. The film was no more accurate historically than the 1973 version by John Milius, but as the first film to be named explicitly after a real-life gangster, it became a huge box-office success.

Center and bottom left: Warren Oates as John Dillinger with gang members dead and alive in two scenes from the 1973 version. Oates was perhaps the perfect actor for the part: similar in appearance, and with an amiable enough personality to play the desperado who, in fact, may never have actually killed anyone.

Left: The real Baby Face Nelson laid out on the slab after being killed by the FBI in the early Thirties. On screen he was played by Mickey Rooney in Don Siegel's 1958 biopic, and by Richard Dreyfuss in 1973.

maddened and slowly destroyed by syphilis.

More impressive were Robert Aldrich's **The Grissom Gang** (1971), an effectively sordid remake of James Hadley Chase's vintage tale of kidnapping, *No Orchids for Miss Blandish,* in which the mother-dominated family that hi-jacks heiress Kim Darby reveals a sexual and psychological perversity that more than equals Ma Barker's brood; and Terrence Malick's **Badlands** (1974),an emotionally cool and perceptive account of two bored young people (Martin Sheen and Sissy Spacek) indulging in a futile killing spree during the Fifties. Shot with the same visual splendor that marked Malick's later **Days of Heaven** (1978), the film refuses to glamorize the pair, and contrasts the banality of their lives and ideas with the romantic stories offered by the movies and magazines of the time.

Romance and remakes

A similar strategy of contrasting real life with media versions lies at the heart of Robert Altman's **Thieves Like Us** (1974), taken from the same novel as Nicholas Ray's **They Live By Night** and telling almost exactly the same story as the earlier film. Although it again treats the central couple of Bowie (Keith Carradine) and Keechie (Shelley Duvall) as naive innocents, it never romanticizes them, but views them as none-too-bright participants in a world that promises more than it can give.

The couple's fumbling love-making is touchingly accompanied by a florid radio version of *Romeo and Juliet*; the gang's clumsy bank-robbing activities are offset by dramatic radio serials like *The Shadow* and *Gangbusters*; newspaper accounts invariably report their exploits with erroneous extravagance. Living in such a society, it is none too surprising that the small-time gangsters are deluded into thinking of themselves as heroic desperadoes en route to fame and fortune. Altman never makes excuses for his characters, but he does sympathize with their plight; the result is one of the most touching and intelligent gangster films of the Seventies.

The glamorous myth-making of **Bonnie and Clyde** was developed even further in John Milius' **Dillinger** (1973). Historical facts are ignored and distorted as Dillinger (Warren Oates) and G-Man Melvin Purvis (Ben Johnson) square up to each other for an epic battle to the death, both seemingly aware of their future inclusion in the Criminal Hall of Fame. An interesting modern biography could be made about Dillinger (there is even some doubt as to whether the man killed outside the Chicago cinema in 1934 was really the notorious gangster), but Milius is uninterested in factual truth.

His characters are the Gangster and Lawman as Legend, figures who by their very nature expose the artificiality of movie conceptions of famous men as lone all-powerful individuals set apart from the rest of society. Stylish, amoral, and sparkling with tongue-in-cheek wit, **Dillinger** also benefits from a strong cast that includes Richard Dreyfuss as the self-destructive Baby Face Nelson.

A woman's view

The rural gangster film would seem to have died out in recent years, although one exception deserves honorable mention. **The Lady in Red** (1979), based very loosely indeed on the real-life figures of Polly Franklin (or Hamilton) and of Anna Sage, the Rumanian immigrant cajoled by the FBI into betraying Dillinger, uses the conventions of the gangster film to reassess women's position in American crime history. Though she takes over the red (actually orange) dress worn by Anna, Polly

Far left: Rod Steiger in the title role of the first screen biography of the most famous hoodlum in American history, **Al Capone** (1959). The film was a surprisingly somber affair. *Inset:* The real life Capone under indictment in Chicago Federal Court.

The St Valentine's Day Massacre (1967).
Below: A dramatic shot of the St Valentine's Day gangland murder on February 14th 1929.

Bottom: Jason Robards Jr as Al Capone. Physically, only the tell-tale scar bore any resemblance to the real Capone, although the film was factually accurate, depicting even violent events like Capone laying into a treacherous hood with a baseball bat.

(Pamela Sue Martin) is no treacherous moll; rather, as a lifetime of hardship and oppression forces her through a succession of sleazy, demeaning jobs – sweat-shop seamstress, taxi-driver, prostitute in the brothel run by Anna (Louise Fletcher) – she acquires a strength, confidence and independence that transform her from passive victim to active defender of her rights. The film's final distortion of the truth is triumphant in tone: the fictional Polly avenges the death of her gangster-lover by turning to robbery herself, leading a gang of similarly disillusioned unfortunates into crime and violent death. Fast, funny and full of spicy social comment, the movie was disappointing only in its lack of commercial success.

In spite of the televised revelations of mafioso-turned-informer Joseph Valachi in 1963, which confirmed and elucidated the existence and organization of the Mafia, the Italian-dominated Syndicate had as such rarely been depicted or even named in the movies. With Civil Rights movements becoming increasingly powerful during the Sixties, Hollywood was probably afraid not only of Mob reprisals (the film industry was not immune to the influence of the underworld) but also of alienating the sympathies of sensitive audiences who might claim that Italian-Americans were being denigrated. (To this day many stand by their denial of the Mafia's existence in America, thanks partly to the influence in the early Seventies of the Italian-American Civil Rights League founded by Joe Colombo, who turned out to be the head of one of New York's Mafia families.)

In 1968, however, Kirk Douglas and Alex Cord starred as two warring brothers who were joint-bosses of **The Brotherhood**, fighting it out to the death over whether or not the Mob should update itself and involve itself in narcotics. Although it showed many of the Mafia's rituals – particularly the Kiss of Death planted on a victim before he is killed – the world was not ready for such unsavory goings-on and the film flopped.

The Godfathers
In 1972, however, Francis Ford Coppola's **The Godfather**, based on Mario Puzo's best-selling book, was so successful that a

Far left: Femme fatale from the farmlands. Pamela Sue Martin as Polly Franklin in **The Lady in Red** (1979), a witty and to some extent feminist account of a woman who reacts to her lover John Dillinger's death by turning to crime.

Left: Kiss of Death. Kirk Douglas as the Mafia Godfather performing a ritual started by Judas and taken up by the Mob, in one of the first movies to mention explicitly the Mafia, **The Brotherhood** (1968).

Below: Arch-heavy henchman of the Corleone clan Luca Brasi (Lenny Montana) receives a knife through the hand and a garotte round the neck in **The Godfather**, made by Francis Ford Coppola in 1972.

Lepke (X)

**THE KING
OF MURDER INC.**

Left: Tony Curtis in the title role of **Lepke** (1974), based on the rise to power of Louis "Lepke" Buchalter, from being a thug for the protection rackets surrounding the garment industry, to becoming head of "Murder Inc", the Mob's murder squad. The film ended with his death in the electric chair in 1944.

Right: During the lavish wedding party at the start of **The Godfather**, Don Vito Corleone (Marlon Brando) gives an audience to a mere minion seeking help. Brando's performance was a tour-de-force and its quiet strength contributed greatly to the sense of honor and dignity which Coppola attributed to the Corleones.

sequel (**The Godfather Part II**) followed in 1974.

Together, the films focus on the rise and rise of one particular family – the Corleones – from young Vito's arrival in New York from Sicily at the start of the century to his death as an old man and his youngest son Michael's appearance before a Senate investigation into organized crime in the Sixties.

Coppola concentrates on the world of the Corleones – the word Mafia is never mentioned – to the exclusion of the world outside; his purpose was to use the Mafia as a symbol of corporate, capitalist America in general. Early struggles to survive in New York's Little Italy turn young Vito (Robert De Niro), who seeks "respect" and has to defend his "honor" into a small-time killer and protection racketeer; slowly but steadily, the family business expands and expands until by the time Michael (Al Pacino) has taken over as boss from his father (played in old age by Marlon Brando), he is reigning over an enormous crime empire less concerned with honor, vendetta and protection than with money, politics and the maintenance of absolute power.

The film in fact is very much about the corruption of ideals by the abuse of power, and as such concentrates less on violence than on sinister conversations whispered in darkened rooms and shifting relationships between the Corleones and their associates in crime. To this end, the movie – counting both parts, it lasts over six hours – dispenses with the manic energy and speed traditional in gangster films and becomes a slow-moving, meditative soap-opera embellished with sporadic bursts of explicitly gory violence.

All in the Family

The similarity of the film to soap-opera, however, extends beyond its relative lack of action to the attitude taken towards its criminal characters. The Mafia *is* the world; with the significant exception of Michael's second wife, Kay (Diane Keaton), non-mafiosi turn up only rarely, and when they do appear it is as sketchily drawn outsiders – usually corrupt cops and politicians. For all their villainy, the Corleone clan members are presented as respectable, honorable citizens, standing by the traditional

virtues of home, family, respect for one's elders, honesty, trust.

The film rarely deals with how exactly they make their money; involvement in narcotics, prostitution, illegal gambling, and labor-racketeering are effectively glossed over, while the film suggests that Mob-violence only harms Mob-members or corrupt public officials; innocent victims are never seen to be harmed. Mob corruption and brutality are seen as strictly a Family affair.

This disregard for how organized crime affects America at large in real life enables Coppola to engage and hold our sympathies, to present his lethal gangsters as tarnished, troubled but essentially righteous members of a gloriously exotic dynasty who harm no-one but each other; their poisonous power is anesthetized and estheticized. **The Godfather** has been called a gangster film for people who don't enjoy gangster films; the evil on view is too elegant, ordered and honorable to be really troubling.

It may nevertheless be churlish to carp at a film that offers so many pleasures, and which is so clearly the work of ambitious intelligence. Certainly it is full of impressive performances (from De Niro, Brando, Pacino, Robert Duvall, James Caan, John Cazale among others) and beautifully composed images (particularly in De Niro's early scenes in turn-of-the-century New York, notable for precise period reconstruction). And when the talking stops and the violence begins, the film manages – if not to excite – to impress by the sheer scale of the conception.

The Godfather's importance becomes clear when it is compared to its several imitators. **The Valachi Papers** (1972), with Charles Bronson as the real-life mafioso who spilled the beans to the FBI, is badly organized in its dramatization of factual events; while both **The Don Is Dead** (1973), with Anthony Quinn as a Mafia boss, and **Lepke** (1974), with Tony Curtis as real-life mobster "Lepke" Buchalter, are flat, uninspired efforts, relying on the florid depiction of ritual violence and codes of honor, but assembled without a hint of Coppola's stylistic assurance.

A background of vice

It was probably the relative failure of these films to match both the artistic quality and the box-office appeal of Coppola's epic that ensured that the Mafia movie died out almost as quickly as it had arrived. Organized crime has, however, served as a backdrop to a number of fascinating films: in **Mikey and Nicky** (1977) John Cassavetes prowls neon-lit streets accompanied by his old pal Peter Falk only to learn that he is being fingered for a hit-man (Ned Beatty) for betraying the Mob; in **The Gambler** (1974) James Caan owes so much money to loan-sharks that eventually his life is in serious danger; and in **Blue Collar** (1978) a trio of small-time crooks rob their union safe and discover that the union is bound up with organized crime.

Moreover, in a succession of conspiracy thrillers in the mid-Seventies – **The Parallax View** (1974), **Three Days of The Condor, The Killer Elite** (both 1975) and **All The President's Men** (1976) – organized crime was equated with the CIA and politicians. Perhaps the finest, most explicit films to deal with crime as a backdrop to everyday life, however, are Martin Scorsese's **Mean Streets** (1973) and **Raging Bull** (1980).

Like much of **The Godfather, Mean Streets** takes place in Little Italy. Charlie (Harvey Keitel) and Johnny Boy (Robert De Niro) are friends, both operating on the fringes of the Italian-American underworld. The film makes perfectly clear how the mobsters make their money – protection-racketeering around pool-halls and seedy bars, fleecing young innocents who come into the neighborhood in search of drugs. Strictly small-time crime, maybe, at the lowest rungs of the Mob ladder, but Scorsese depicts it with color, wit and intelligence, and never shies away from portraying the violent side-effects of such criminal activity.

When Johnny Boy fails to pay loan-shark Michael (Richard Romanus) both the money he owes him and the respect that Michael feels is his due from a small-time punk, life becomes cheap indeed, and considerations of honor, family and friendship no longer matter. Charlie, Johnny and Johnny's cousin/Charlie's girlfriend Theresa (Amy Robinson) attempt to get out of New York, but the deadly vengeance of the Mob follows them into the anonymity of Brooklyn and falls down upon them in the form of a hired gunman (played, incidentally, by Scorsese himself).

The paranoia of violence

Mean Streets impresses through all those qualities that **The Godfather** shunned – pace, energy, violence and a sense of streetlife irredeemably tainted by corruption from above, with innocent victims threatened by injury and death just as much as the mobsters themselves. And through the acting – particularly De Niro's breathlessly manic performance – Scorsese stresses the dangerously irrational mentality that lies behind the habitual use of violence.

Mean Streets was a step forward in the depiction of urban crime, and the director went on to make increasingly mature and perceptive movies about the paranoid psychology of violence: **Taxi Driver** (1976), **New York, New York** (1977) and most impressively **Raging Bull,** which deals with the poisonous and corrupting effect of organized crime upon the world of boxing.

During the second half of the Seventies, the gangster movie seemed to be in danger of extinction again. Criminal heroes were replaced by cops and vigilantes, alongside disco-dancers, spacemen and aliens, and psychopathic murderers. An increasingly conservative America was looking to less disturbing heroes for comfort. But the mobsters had disappeared from screens before – in the Forties and early Sixties – and had resurfaced. In the Eighties they would return once more.

Far left: Sonny Corleone (James Caan) gives vent to his psychotic temper in **The Godfather** after his brother-in-law Carlo (Gianni Russo) has beaten up Sonny's sister. Virtually all the violence in the film was kept within the family, or directed against a small circle of associates and rivals.

Below: Martin Scorsese's **Mean Streets** (1973) looked at the small-time hoods, pimps and pushers operating in New York's Little Italy, a neighborhood the director knew well from personal experience. The film's breathless energy ensured its cult success, and set its two central performers – Harvey Keitel and Robert De Niro – on the path to stardom.

Left: Blood and bullets in the barber shot. A gory scene from **The Valachi Papers** (1972), one of several films which attempted unsuccessfully to cash in on the mystique of the Mafia which had proved so profitable in **The Godfather**. Though based on fact, the film was a clumsy catalogue of endless murders.

Lee Marvin in **The Killers** (1964). In the 1950s he was the archetypal villain, tough and lean, but he became his own counterpart in the 1960s, now playing the all-conquering hero in cinema and television series alike.

The G-Men Fight Back

The movies have always relied for success on their appeal to people's fantasy lives. Whether dealing in horror, romance, sci-fi or crime, they function like keyholes that offer secret views into forbidden rooms; the audience takes great pleasure in seeing – and to some extent experiencing – what it cannot do in real life, and what it dare not do. Hardly surprising, then, that gangsters should be so appealing to so many – especially in the form in which Hollywood tends to glamorize them – whereas the law enforcement officer, whether a cop, an FBI agent or a Treasury investigator operates in a world that, morally at least, bears far more resemblance to our own.

But the hoodlum hasn't always had it all his own way in the movies. After the overwhelming horde of gangster pictures produced by Hollywood between 1930 and 1934, the good guys fought their way back to center-screen. Perhaps both audiences and studio-heads were tired of the endlessly repetitive formulas in the dozens of crime films made each year following the success of **Little Caesar.**

But other factors contributed to the gangster's downfall. Pressures from various outraged groups concerned about America's moral health resulted, in 1934, in the Motion Picture Producers and Distributors of America tightening the restrictions of the Hays Code concerning the movies' depiction of crime and violence; crime must not be celebrated, let alone seen to pay. Added to this stricter censorship was the fact that, with Roosevelt's arrival as President, the Prohibition laws had been repealed in 1933.

Gangsters, made rich and powerful by bootlegging, could therefore no longer rely on booze as their chief source of income, and depended instead on gambling, narcotics, prostitution, loan-sharking and labor-racketeering for profits. The last two practices were probably deemed unsuitable as subject-matter for movies, being both complex and relatively undramatic, while the Hays Code firmly vetoed drugs and commercial sex as acceptable cinema fodder.

The FBI under Hoover

But a third very important factor came into play in transforming law-enforcers from faceless finks hanging out on the sidelines of the underworld to full-scale heroes: the rise to power and fame of the Federal Bureau of Investigation under the image-conscious leadership of J. Edgar Hoover. The Bureau was given increased legal powers in the early Thirties – including the right

of agents to carry guns – and Hoover won enormous publicity with the FBI's successes in running to ground and killing a number of notorious Public Enemies. These were not, however, the immensely influential hoods that lorded it over city gang-warfare, but far less organized small-timers such as Dillinger, Baby Face Nelson, Bonnie and Clyde, and Machine Gun Kelly. Far less dangerous than organized crime, these minor figures nevertheless became household names, partly because of their own desire for fame (Bonnie Parker wrote poems, others sent letters to the newspapers), partly because Hoover's publicity machine carefully suppressed information about FBI failures and proudly and loudly trumpeted its triumphs. For decades, Hoover denied the existence of organized crime in America, and the Bureau accordingly never ventured to tackle the problem.

According to the Bureau's own myth-making, it was Machine Gun Kelly – in reality a small-time kidnapper, both cowardly and non-violent – who supplied the title for Hollywood's first major celebration of the FBI. When agents, hitherto known as "feds", cornered him, he is said to have screamed, "Don't shoot, G-Men!" The Bureau – ignoring the fact that it was the Memphis police and not the FBI who had really arrested Kelly – keenly explained that this was common criminal slang for "government men", and a dynamic new name was coined.

Machine gunning to victory

G-Men was therefore Hollywood's response in 1935 to pressures both from censorship bodies and from Hoover's FBI. And who better to star in the tale of a brave and efficient gun-totin' agent than the man who had made his name as the most fiery, aggressive, and energetic of mobsters? Indeed, with James Cagney playing Brick Davis, the punk from the wrong side of the tracks who makes good with the Bureau, it was sometimes hard to tell whether the star had truly reformed.

Violence rather than moral worth was emphasized, with Cagney machine-gunning his way to victory over a murderous gangster and looking almost exactly as he had done in earlier criminal roles – rough, tough, fast and fierce. Brick Davis was also in tune with the ways of the underworld, having originated in the slums, been put through college by an old bootlegger, and generally learned to take care of himself in lawless company. The fact that he is not so very different from the characters he's fighting against is also echoed in his motives for gang-busting: he ends up on the right side of the law because he wants to take revenge on the hood who killed his buddy.

Equally as violent as the frowned-upon gangster pictures before it, **G-Men** was a commercial success, and it was not long before the other great stars who had made a name as mobsters followed Cagney into law-enforcing ways. Edward G. Robinson, while continuing to play gangsters (often in comedies), scored a hit with **Bullets or Ballots** (1936), as a cop who goes undercover to join and nail Barton MacLane's gang; needless to say, since Robinson's cop looks like so many screen-gangsters, he's accepted into the criminal world with little ado! Humphrey Bogart too, riding high on a succession of surly gangster portraits in films like **Petrified Forest** and **Bullets or Ballots** (1936), played a crime-busting District Attorney in **Marked Woman** (1937), loosely based on Special Prosecutor Thomas Dewey, the man who nabbed Lucky Luciano on charges of organizing compulsory prostitution, before returning to gangsterdom in **Racket Busters** (1938)·

G-Men (1935).
Left: Pressurised by moral-watchdog bodies and by Hoover's FBI, Hollywood was forced to turn away from its glorification of power-hungry criminals to celebrate instead the forces of Law and Order. The great irony was that for the leading part in **G-Men** (1935), as Fed agent Brick Davis, James Cagney was chosen – despite his history of playing gangster roles.

Below: Spot the good guy. Hardly surprising that Margaret Lindsay should look a little uncertain about her rescuers when they all look like gangsters. But they are in fact "G-Men".

Top right: Cagney's image here was actually little different from that in his hoodlum pictures. He still snarled, sneered, and spat out his lines, and was no less violent or hot-tempered than when he had been operating on the other side of the law.

Above: Bette Davis as one of a group of (thinly disguised) prostitutes reacting against exploitation by the Mob in **Marked Woman** (1937), based loosely on real-life events: the successful use of informers by Thomas Dewey in his case against Lucky Luciano.

After the war

The Forties being the decade of the private eye and the disillusioned hero, the cop and FBI agent heroes largely disappeared into the shadows along with the gangsters. The All-American Male was now to be seen battling it out against a far greater enemy in Europe and Asia, doing his bit for democracy in the face of Hitler's hordes. Even the FBI was found tracking down Nazi spies in the mean streets of New York in **The House on 92nd Street** (1945), although not surprisingly the enemy agents tend to act and dress like true-blue American hoods.

When, after the War, law-enforcers did resume action against home-grown crime, they were less likely to be straightforward cops than Treasury agents either investigating counterfeiters (**T-Men**, 1948) or tracking down bank-robber Cody Jarrett (**White Heat,** 1949); immigration officials uncovering an organization smuggling foreigners into the States by illegal means (**Border Incident,** 1949); or DAs persuading criminals to become informers (**Kiss of Death,** 1947). Otherwise, it was largely left to the private eye to sort out society by solving isolated crimes.

Two fine films, however, did deal with law-enforcement during the Forties. In 1948, **Cry of the City** saw cop Candella (Victor Mature) pitted against hoodlum Rome (Richard Conte), a long-standing acquaintance from the same Italian neighbourhood. A riveting thriller, the film is also important for a number of reasons. It gave full rein to Conte's quietly menacing and suavely sinister qualities, characteristics that would serve him well in the Fifties when he would become one of the archetypal movie Mob-leaders.

It was also, thanks to the stylish direction of top thriller-maker Robert Siodmak, one of the first gangster movies to make full use of the dense, dark, shadowy camerawork common in private-eye films: streets black and threatening, illuminated here and there by brilliant, isolated pools of light reflected in seemingly never-ending rain. And most importantly, it created a real bond between hero and villain. Not only are Candella and Rome old friends who just happen to have gone separate ways; they even seem like positive/negative reflections of one another, with the cop always dressed in a black raincoat and the gangster in white. It is as if they are locked together in an eternal struggle for power which defies human logic, a theme that would be taken up in many later thrillers, perhaps most notably with Clint Eastwood in **Dirty Harry** (1971) and **Tightrope** (1984).

The Undercover Man

The other major law vs gangster movie of the decade, **The Undercover Man** (1949), impresses through its realism. Inspired by the Capone case (the Big Fellow of the movie is prosecuted for tax evasion), it concerns federal Treasury agent Glenn Ford who not only hunts down his victim by physical pursuit but also gains his evidence through bureaucracy, wading through piles of paperwork. And unlike most crime-thrillers concerning mobsters, both before and since, the film actually shows that gang violence affects not just cops and other hoods but everyone; witnesses to crimes are silenced, and even during a stunning chase innocent passers-by are involved, with the danger symbolized by the face of a little girl, shocked and horrified as a gangster is finally killed before her very eyes.

After the rather feeble Forties, the Fifties arrived like a breath of not exactly fresh air for both hoods and cops. In 1950-1, the Kefauver Committee had confirmed and publicized the existence of organized crime, opening the way for a new style of crime film. And just as the mobsters themselves were depicted with a new interest in psychology and wide-spread corruption,

so the law enforcers were shown in a rather more complex light than their predecessors.

First up in the organized crime stakes was **The Enforcer** with Humphrey Bogart — on almost perpetual leave from his hoodlum image since the success of **The Maltese Falcon** in 1941 — as the investigating DA based loosely on Burton Turkus,

Cry of the City (1948).
Bottom left: Richard Conte as Rome, the Italianate hoodlum.

Right: On the trail of counterfeit money in **T-Men** (1948).

Bottom right: Cop Candella falling out with Rome.

Below left: A brutal scene from **Murder Inc.** (1960).

the man who had exposed "Murder, Inc" as the Syndicate's contractual "hit"-squad. Introduced by Senator Kefauver himself, the film in time-honored fashion concentrates more on the Mob's activities than on law-enforcement. But the portrait of the good guy is still interesting in that, unlike Cagney's G-Man, he can't go around restoring law and order with a tommy-gun and semi-criminal tactics. Also, since it is the Syndicate rather than one lone mobster who is the enemy, Bogart has difficulty in getting his case to stick: accidents happen, witnesses disappear.

Freud hits the screen
For all Bogart's talents, the film's focus ensures that the figure of the attorney is relatively traditional and two-dimensional. But Hollywood's newly found interest in Freud was bound to affect even a genre as action-packed as the gangster movie, and cops began to suffer from severe psychological hang-ups.

A film like **The Narrow Margin** (1952), which deals with cop Charles McGraw escorting a gangster's widow (Marie Windsor) by train to give evidence against the Mob, seems on the surface to be merely a neat, if extremely gripping, little thriller with original plot twists. But unlike most cops before him, McGraw is a far from sympathetic character; full of contempt for the woman he's ordered to protect, his bitterness (proved even more objectionable when he – and we – learn that she is really a police decoy) derives from an almost psychopathic hatred of law-breakers – and, one suspects, sassy women.

Even more irrational and dangerous is Robert Ryan in Nicholas Ray's **On Dangerous Ground** (1952), a true forerunner to Dirty Harry in his cynicism and maddened violence towards any small-time punk he encounters. His brutality in arresting and getting confessions from criminals prompts him into an argument with his partner:

Ryan: "Garbage, that's all we handle. Garbage! How do you live with it?"

Partner: "I *don't* live with it. I live with other people."

Ryan's predicament – he has become so emotionally and psychologically worn out by the crime and corruption around him that he acts like a vicious avenging angel, using methods little different from the criminals he's pursuing – is echoed increasingly in later movies. In **The Big Heat,** Sergeant Dave Bannion (Glenn Ford) seems the only cop honest and courageous enough to take on the power of Lagana's city-wide Mob; the rest of the police force are either too afraid or have been corrupted. And yet Bannion's efforts are hardly whitewashed heroics; he becomes motivated to ever more desperate extremes after his wife is killed by a car-bomb intended for him, and actually gives up his badge – the seal of his authority – rather than give up his desire for revenge. He uses people unfeelingly, and seems forever on the brink of killing someone out of maddened outrage rather than a sense of justice. His lack of interest in the law limits our capacity to

Above: Embittered cop Charles McGraw (with gun) gets his man, an assassin hired to kill a woman about to testify against the Syndicate, in **The Narrow Margin** (1952).

Left: Crime-buster as clerk. Ferguson (Humphrey Bogart) uses records rather than revolvers to nail the murderous men at the top of the criminal heap, in **The Enforcer** (1951).

Right: Rogue-cop Jim Wilson (Robert Ryan) deals with what he considers the human "garbage" he is forced to deal with during his daily grind, in Nicholas Ray's psychological police-thriller **On Dangerous Ground** (1952).

Below: Obese bent cop Hank Quinlan (Orson Welles) frames Joe Grande (Akim Tamiroff) for abducting Susan Vargas (Janet Leigh). Welles' **Touch of Evil** (1958) is one of the most complex explorations of law and justice ever filmed.

Right: Cody Jarrett (James Cagney) and undercover agent Hank Fallon (Edmond O'Brien) – pretending to be a hardened convict to gain Jarrett's trust – decide to take a break from prison life in Raoul Walsh's **White Heat** (1949).

Bottom right: Clues from shoes. District Attorney Ferguson (Bogart) sifts through the sole evidence remaining of Murder Inc's various victims, in **The Enforcer** (1951).

sympathize fully with him as a safe and trustworthy enforcer and protector of society.

World of corruption

Corrupt or psychologically tormented cops appear repeatedly in the Fifties. In **The Big Combo**, cop Cornel Wilde puts the heat on mobster Richard Conte not so much out of a desire that justice be done as out of sexual jealousy; Wilde, at the start of the film indulging in a casual, rather callous affair with a doting stripper, is inflamed by the fact that the respectable, "nice" girl he adores (Jean Wallace) is Conte's mistress.

In his own **Touch of Evil** (1958), Orson Welles plays the bloated, bigoted and extremely respected police detective Hank Quinlan, an aging and successful grotesque who is not averse to framing innocents or even killing a fellow-cop to prove his hunches correct and keep his reputation intact. Law-enforcing heroes, in fact, had become more recognizably human, with feelings and fears and faults. Only in the belated celebration of **The FBI Story** (1959) were clean-cut heroes again worshipped; not surprisingly, the film seems insufferably dull in comparison to its more complex, colorful and cynical counterparts.

With few gangster movies being made in the first half of the Sixties, interesting cops also kept a low profile. And even in the later years of the decade, the crooks still seemed to have the upper hand; after all, this was the time of Liberation, Freedom and anti-establishment attitudes. Among the younger generations, at least, cops were regarded as "pigs". Only supercool Steve McQueen as **Bullitt** (1968) really left a mark on audiences, and that was more for his cool blue eyes and driving abilities in the superbly crafted chase sequences than for any strength of personality.

The sole truly interesting depiction of the police world was in Don Siegel's **Madigan.** Made the same year as **Bullitt** but far more concerned with the dilemmas facing cops in an increasingly violent world, it reveals a society where

Below: Madigan (Richard Widmark) looks downcast as his methods are again criticised by his liberal but uncomprehending superior (Henry Fonda). The film's study of the conflict between idealism and compromise in police methods made it a predecessor to Siegel's later **Dirty Harry** (1971).

compromise is the norm, where Madigan (Richard Widmark) is criticized for his methods by superiors who nevertheless expect him to solve cases in double-quick time. Harassed on all sides, forced into situations where he has to shoot first and ask questions later, Madigan is the prototype for the far more violent and disturbing incarnations of police morality in **The French Connection** and **Dirty Harry**, both made in 1971.

Popeye takes to heroin
In **The French Connection** (1971), Gene Hackman's foul-mouthed Popeye Doyle is on the trail of mobsters smuggling heroin from Marseilles to New York. As played by Hackman in a virtuoso performance, he's a recognizably flawed human being – bigoted, hot-tempered, he even shoots a federal agent by mistake. But his sheer determination to succeed and the fact that he leads an unglamorous life in a seedy, sordid world play on audience sympathies. How can we not appreciate the efforts of a man who just never gives up, who is reduced to eating takeaway pizzas in the street when the villains he is after are enjoying a wonderful gourmet lunch? And yet Popeye is also given to outbursts of racist abuse, to brutal violence that goes way beyond the call of duty.

It is perhaps because of this confusion on the film's part as to whether or not he is a hero to be admired that the focus lies more with atmosphere (grimy New York backstreets) and action (particularly the celebrated lengthy car-chase) than with human qualities.

"The Law's crazy"
Dirty Harry, though an even more troubled film, at least confronts the ethics of police violence head on. Harry Callahan (Clint Eastwood) gets results – but he does so by methods that sidestep the letter of the law and infuriate his bosses, the mayor and seemingly liberal-minded lawyers. He in turn is infuriated by them, and when Scorpio (Andy Robinson), the manic sniper killing innocent San Franciscans left, right and center, is set free because Harry (by torturing him for information about a kidnapped girl) has not respected his rights during an arrest, Harry scowls, "The Law's crazy". The cop in fact turns out to be virtually a vigilante, equipped with a huge .44 Magnum and with a deep, cynical hatred for what he considers to be the scum element of the city.

Siegel's film is profoundly ambiguous concerning Harry's courage, professionalism and methods. On the one hand, he is regarded as possessing almost superhuman powers (several symbols serve to equate him, ironically, with Jesus), while a madman like Scorpio should surely be prevented from causing more carnage; on the other, at several key points in the film, Siegel stresses a parallel between the hunter and his prey. The only difference, it seems, is that Harry carries a badge although the film's ending has him toss this into a river after he has finally killed the sniper.

Does this mean that he recognizes that he has gone beyond the acceptable limits of law enforcement? Or does he feel such contempt for the liberal attitudes and bureaucracy of the system that he wants nothing more to do with it? The film itself offers no easy answers, although the fact that Eastwood reinstated Harry in the Police Department in several sequels (**Magnum Force**, 1973; **The Enforcer**, 1976; and **Sudden Impact**, 1983) suggest that the star at least felt he may only have gone a little too far in his pursuit of duty.

Sudden Impact, however, not only gives Harry a halo as he battles it out with a group of ludicrously depicted villains, but also allows him the power of a judge; having discovered that Sondra Locke is a mass-killer, he lets her go free because she

acts on vigilante ideas similar to his own.

Police problems
Less objectionable and far more interesting was **Tightrope** in which Eastwood forsook Harry altogether and played a New Orleans cop, Wes Block, who in tracking down a sex-killer, realizes that his own sadistic treatment of women makes him

Left: Clint Eastwood examines a drowned body in **Tightrope** (1984).

Right: Narcotics detective Danny Ciello (Treat Williams) testifies in court in Sidney Lumet's epic **Prince of the City** (1981).

Bottom left: Mask of madness. Inspector Harry Callahan (Clint Eastwood) comes face to face with his alter-ego Scorpio (Andy Robinson) in **Dirty Harry** (1971).

Below: Inspector Harry Callahan, back on his feet and in hot pursuit in **Dirty Harry**.

Bottom right: Needled narc Popeye Doyle (Gene Hackman) takes aim in **The French Connection 2** (1976).

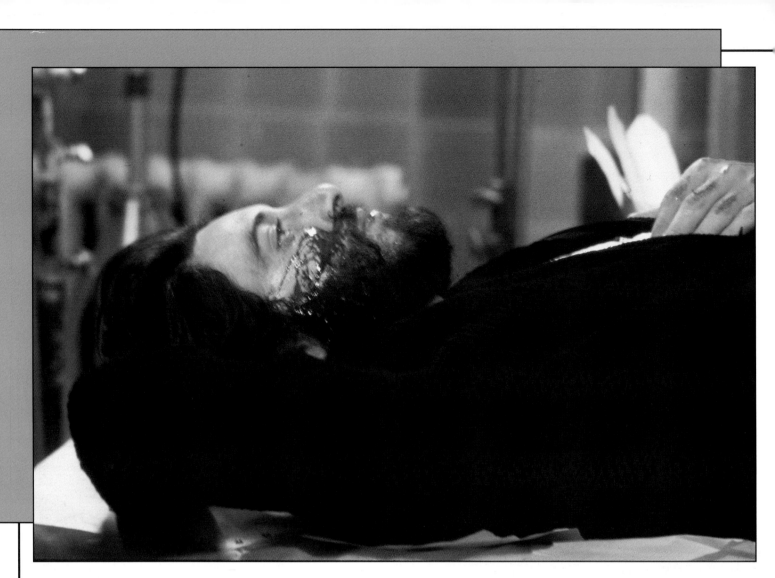

not so very different from the murderer. The film reveals the star at his most ambitious and self-critical. In a long line of roles in which Eastwood has repeatedly presented himself as the most morally and psychologically anguished of screen cops, **Tightrope** is possibly the most adventurous yet.

The other side of the coin to the Dirty Harry films and other movies portraying the vigilante ethic (including numerous Charles Bronson movies, following the success of the hysterical **Death Wish,** 1974) lies with the conspiracy thrillers. In these films, either organized crime has fully infiltrated the police department, or the police departments have simply taken a leaf out of the Mob's book and are thoroughly corrupt, indulging in full-scale cover-ups. In two movies by Sidney Lumet, **Serpico** (1974) and **Prince of the City** (1981), one is almost led to believe that the incorruptible heroes (whiter-than-white Al Pacino and a more ambiguous Treat Williams respectively) are the sole examples of law-abiding cops in all New York.

Both find themselves surrounded by colleagues at every level taking bribes, turning blind eyes, generally indulging in petty crime and rake-offs; and when they threaten to spill the beans on the widespread corruption they so dislike, they find themselves faced with potential witnesses who refuse to talk and with angrily self-protective officers who will do anything – even kill – to protect themselves.

The films are at once cynical in the depiction of police departments in which honesty is almost unknown, and impeccably liberal in their support of individuals who believe that, whatever the circumstances, cops should always abide by the book without taint of suspicion. It is perhaps no accident that Frank Serpico – based on a real-life character – is notable not

only for his honesty but also for his hippie-like appearance; in this and his generally eccentric ways, he could hardly be accused by Seventies audiences of being a typical "pig". He was too much like themselves.

Cops in general, however, emerged severely tainted during the Seventies. No longer were they clean-cut American heroes. In times when people expect the police to protect them from crime but at the same time often detest those individuals who actually take on that task, it is natural that movie cops should be presented as far from perfect. Police violence on the screen reached its apogee in **Across 110th Street** (1972) in which Anthony Quinn, investigating mob warfare, plays an aging detective given to taking bribes, insulting his black partner (Yaphet Kotto), and doling out brutal physical punishment.

Less extreme examples, such as Richard Jordan in **The Friends of Eddie Coyle**, Bruce Dern in **The Driver** (1978) and Nick Nolte in **48 Hours** (1982) are still far from totally sympathetic, honest characters. J. Edgar Hoover, so concerned that lawmen should be shown as paragons of purity, would have been deeply shocked and disgusted by the way we now view upholders of the law. But even he, the most famed, vainglorious and discreet of crime-busters was finally revealed in **The Private File of J. Edgar Hoover** (1978) as a sexually repressed self-seeker, involved in political wheeling and dealing, manipulating enormous cover-ups of corruption in high places, and generally operating in a less than absolutely legal manner.

In times where we are no longer able to put our faith in the infallibility of the head of the FBI, when corruption seems all-pervading and inevitable, it has become increasingly difficult to distinguish exactly between the good guys and the bad guys.

Left: Frank Serpico (Al Pacino) rewarded with his cheek shot through, after making an honest stand against corruption in the force, in Sidney Lumet's **Serpico** (1974).

48 Hours, Walter Hill's slick mixture of action and wisecracking comedy.
Below left: Nick Nolte as grouchy, growling detective Jack Cates.

Bottom: The odd couple. Cop Cates teams up with convict Reggie Hammond (Eddie Murphy), freed from prison to help catch a couple of kidnappers.

Below right: Cates squeezes a little co-operation out of small-time villain Luther (David Patrick Kelly).

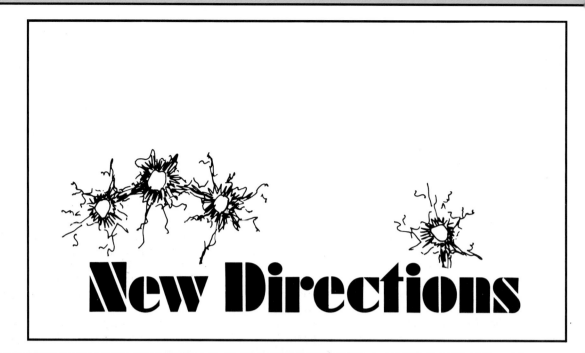

New Directions

Fighting dirty deeds back in the Thirties, Lieutenant Speer (Clint Eastwood) stops at nothing – not even when bullets come wailing through the windscreen, as in **City Heat** (1984).

Fashions in both film-making and moviegoing in the Eighties are very different from those of half a century ago. During the heyday of the first major gangster movies, Hollywood was producing many hundreds of films each year, and a large proportion of Western society was responding to this enormous output by visiting the cinema as often as once a week. The medium was still young, confident and universally popular.

Now, however, cinemas offer just one of several forms of visual entertainment. Film's sovereignty has been severely diminished by the introduction, over the years, of television, cable and video. Many people (more in Britain than the USA) now visit a cinema only once or twice a year, some even less frequently. In the struggle to hold on to audiences, the movie industry has resorted more and more to big "event" films; fewer films are being made each year, and the business relies largely on a few successful mega-hits to keep the profits flowing. Another major change lies in the nature of the audience.

Filmgoing used to be a family affair; now the audience consists to an enormous extent of people aged under 25. Hollywood therefore directs its product more and more at the youth market. Over the last decade, **Star Wars**, **Saturday Night Fever** (both 1977) and **Halloween** (1978) have set fashions for incredibly repetitive formula grind-outs: endless carbon-copy teen-movies dealing with mindlessly entertaining, spectacular sci-fi, gory tales of barely human monsters mass-murdering gangs of fun-lovin' kids, and disco or breakdance travesties of the old rags-to-riches, puttin'-on-a show musicals. Other kinds of film have had a harder time of it; some, like the Western (for decades the most reliably popular genre), virtually became temporarily extinct.

New style gangsters

The result of this sorry state of affairs, bred by the marriage of changing audience patterns with the introduction into studio-head jobs of corporate businessmen interested more in making deals than in making movies, has been a lack of direction, a lack of faith in the ability of the old formulas to keep a hold on film-goers. The gangster film in the Eighties is by and large a very different creature from those of the Thirties and Fifties (which is not necessarily to say it is any worse).

In addition to the changes in the movie world, this may also be partly due to a common conception of crime and violence in the modern world. Romantic anti-hero figures like Capone and

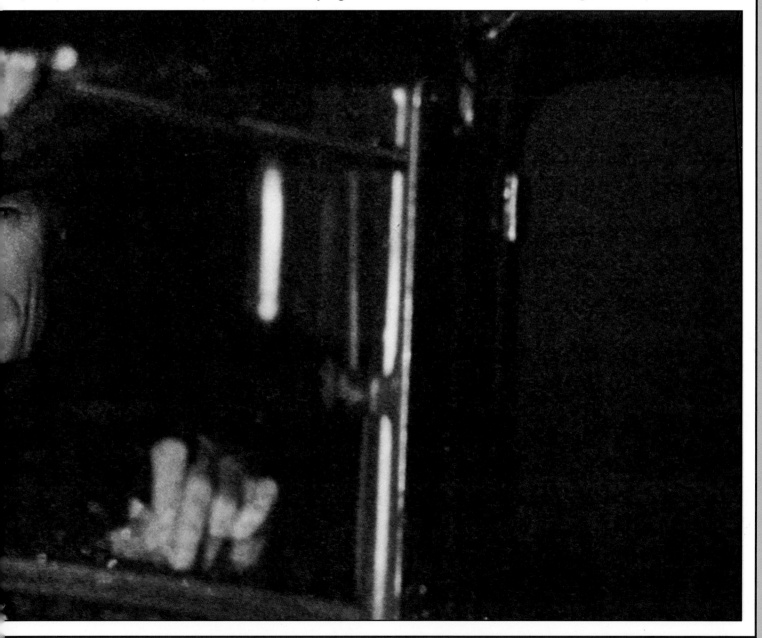

Dillinger are no more; organized crime has become so faceless, so outwardly respectable, so integral a part of contemporary society that it may even be invisible to the undiscerning eye. Rather, modern crime often seems to be thought of as a messy mass of isolated events perpetrated by antisocial, irresponsible individuals.

The mugging in the street, not the bank-robbery or the Mob-murder, would seem to be the crime of the Eighties. Hardly surprising, then, that the most common and popular of crime-movies these days seem to be the vigilante movies, such as those starring Charles Bronson.

The gangster movie has, however, survived; and although only a relatively small number have been made in the Eighties, their imaginative and original quality has often been so strong that the genre seems assured of continuing popularity. It is, however, increasingly difficult to speak of mobster movies as a tight genre; perhaps only Brian De Palma's **Scarface** (1983) and Sergio Leone's **Once Upon a Time in America** (1984) fit snugly into the same category as the traditional gangster epics of yesteryear. Other recent excursions into the underworld have dealt with crime only, as it were, in passing, showing as much interest in non-criminal elements of the story.

Gloria: Moll with a mission

A characteristic and excellent example of the way gangster-movie motifs can be adapted to other purposes is John Cassavetes' **Gloria** (1980). The hard and brassy dame of the title, played by Cassavetes' wife, Gena Rowlands, is a gangster's ex-mistress living in modern New York. One of her neighbors, Buck Henry, is an accountant for the Mob; to protect himself he is threatening to reveal the contents of a little ledger-book dealing with illegal activities. The Mob retaliates by killing Henry and his family, and Gloria is saddled with the sole survivor from the explosion, the accountant's precocious eight-year-old son.

Gloria, it seems, has little in the way of maternal instincts, and she does her kindly best to get rid of the boy — until, that is, the gangsters decide to kill him, since the kid has the incriminating ledger-book in his possession. As Gloria protects him from the ruthless gunmen, she gradually discovers that her relationship with the boy is valuable, and revises her opinions of her underworld friends, whom she soon comes to regard as unnaturally heartless killers.

Cassavetes' movie is certainly a great thriller, and it does indeed trade in the symbols that have distinguished gangster

Scarface
Above: Paul Muni as Tony Camonte in Howard Hawks' original **Scarface** (1932). Less foul-mouthed than Pacino's later incarnation, he also managed to peddle booze without becoming an alcoholic, whereas Montana, in the remake, became a fully-fledged cocaine-addict.

Left: Tony Montana (Al Pacino), a Cuban exile washed up on the shores of the Miami coast, makes the most of the American Dream by riding to wealth and power on a wave of cocaine smuggling and murder, in Brian De Palma's lengthy, violent remake (1983).

movies for decades: flash limos, sharp clothes, silent thugs, elegant penthouses, guns. And yet the film is far more than just a thriller; it is also an explicit critique of women's traditional roles in the movies.

Rarely if ever before has it been acknowledged that gangsters' molls could have tender feelings, especially for

Below: Gena Rowlands as gangsters' moll **Gloria** (1980), whose dislike of children vanishes when she is forced to look after a neighbor's son whose life is threatened by the Mob.

children. Movie-women have been stereotypically thrust into the roles of either Mother (or Good Girl) or Whore (Bad Girl). **Gloria**'s importance and power lies partly in the way it reveals that these categories are artificial: the Mother and the Whore, the Good Girl and the Bad Girl can and do exist within one and the same person.

The film also makes enormously progressive strides in its depiction of a strong woman who never feels dominated by men: Gloria is tough, independent, quick-witted and streetwise; she handles a gun with speed and accuracy; and in one magnificent scene when she is being threatened by a mobster on the Subway, she lays him out with a punch that might make Joe Louis stagger. Nobody, but nobody, pushes her around; **Gloria** is a joyful celebration of a woman more than holding her own in a man's world.

On the boardwalk

Like Cassavetes' film, Louis Malle's **Atlantic City** (1981) also takes the subject of a lone, unlikely individual facing up to the collective power of the Mob and turns it to its own special purposes. Lou Pascal (Burt Lancaster) is an elderly small-time crook, working a not very profitable numbers game in the poorer backstreets of the New Jersey resort. Obsessed with regaining his youth through an affair with trainee casino croupier Sally (Susan Sarandon), he becomes involved in some dangerous drugs-dealing with her ex-husband, Dave, who has stolen a stash of heroin from the Mob in Philadelphia. The Mob emissaries discover the culprit, Dave is killed, and Lou carries on with his extremely profitable narcotics sales until the thugs finally track him down. When they threaten to kill Sally, the old man actually shoots them dead – to everyone's surprise, but mostly to his own. For a brief moment of glory, he becomes a wanted desperado, caught up in what the television newscasters describe as a full-scale gang war.

The clash between lone hero and Mob hordes is a tried and tested theme in the movies; it was the main impulse in films like **Point Blank** and **The Outfit**. What makes the subject so interesting here is that Lou is an old man whose involvement in danger allows him to manage to escape from his rose-colored memories. Until the confrontation that ends in death, Lou lives permanently in a past that never existed: he claims, falsely, that he once worked for the likes of Capone, Lucky Luciano, Dutch Schultz and Meyer Lansky; that he has killed people; that he was Bugsy Siegel's cellmate (in fact, it turns out that Lou saw Siegel once for a few seconds when locked up on a drunk-and-disorderly charge).

Lou bemoans the rise of large casinos in Atlantic City – "Now it's so goddam legal!" – and even goes so far as to suggest that the Atlantic itself is not what it used to be – "You should've seen the Ocean in those days." The old man is actually out of his depth in the modern world, as much of a relic of the past as the sad, decaying but majestic hotels being demolished on the seafront. He may know how to walk his neighbor's poodle to the pet-shop, but he has no idea, at first, of the value of the drugs Dave shows him. And yet his tender, protective love for Sally and his newly found ability to adapt to a changed world ensure that when the time comes, he can kill; it is something he has always dreamed of doing, and he is revitalized by the act.

Beauty and the Beast

His dignity, his pride in himself, are no longer sham but real; his confidence is restored to such an extent that, at the end of the film, he feels able to let Sally leave him and to return to Grace, his similarly aged girlfriend. At last, he accepts himself and his age. Malle's film does take place in a recognisably real world –

Left: **Gloria** (Gena Rowlands) proves herself a hot-shot as she defends eight-year-old Phil (John Adames) from the heartless members of the Mob sent to kill him. Rowlands' tough performance has rightly been described as like that of a modern, female version of Bogart in his heyday, although never for one moment does she abandon her femininity.

Below: On the boardwalks of **Atlantic City** (1981), aging small-time numbers racketeer Lou Pascal (Burt Lancaster) regains his self-respect by protecting Sally (Susan Sarandon) against murderous Mob reprisals, after she is connected with the theft of a large stash of heroin.

Left: Peering into the past. Lou Pascal (Burt Lancaster) tells tall stories about his criminal life long before he arrived in **Atlantic City.** But only when he is in his seventies does he actually manage to hit the Big Time, kill a gangster, and be credited by the press as starting up a full-scale gang war.

Right: James Caan in mean mood in Michael Mann's **Thief** (1981), a cool, clever thriller about a professional master-burglar whose illegal activities bring him and his girlfriend Tuesday Weld into catastrophic conflict with the Mob.

indeed, the resort is the only gambling haven on the East Coast, a status that has to some extent ensured the arrival in the city of organized crime – but the film uses the setting for metaphorical effect. **Atlantic City** becomes a superb symbol of the way crime has changed over the years, of an old and extravagant order being replaced by something apparently more sterile, faceless and respectable. The story, central to which is the old man's rediscovery of life, joy and self-respect through his relationship with a beautiful young woman, has the quality of a romantic but amoral fairy-tale: a Beauty and the Beast set in the modern Underworld. Merging this poetic, almost fantastic vein with familiar and realistic gangster motifs, the film is without doubt a charming original.

A number of films have used gangsters less centrally and less imaginatively as a backdrop for other concerns. In **Thief*** (1981), maestro-burglar James Caan comes into conflict with fat, sinister mafiosi, but the real focus of the film is on his cool professionalism and his stark commitment to himself, alleviated only by loyalty to his three-time loser buddy Willie Nelson and his lover Tuesday Weld.

The Pope of Greenwich Village (1984) is a rather tame re-run of the **Mean Streets** story, with Mickey Rourke and Eric Roberts as Charlie and Paulie, buddies involved with the fringes of New York's Italian-American underworld; only Burt Young impresses with a charismatic portrait of a menacing mafioso named Bedbug Eddie, threatening to remove Charlie's hand. And even Woody Allen structured a delightful comedy around the conceit of a small-time showbiz agent getting into troubled waters with the Mob after it is thought that he has stolen Mia Farrow from an arranged marriage to one of their number. **Broadway Danny Rose** (1984) is not only one of Allen's most touching comedies; thanks to the presence of the Mob, it is also his most thrilling.

Return of Scarface

These films are, however, comparatively marginal to the gangster genre proper. More traditional in many respects was Brian De Palma's remake of the Howard Hawks-Ben Hecht classic, **Scarface.** What is surprising about the new version is its closeness to the original even though it is twice as long as the Thirties film. Tony Montana (Al Pacino) is a seedy small-time criminal who after being thrown out of Castro's Cuba turns up in Florida and almost immediately becomes mixed up with hoodlums heavily involved in smuggling drugs into America. Montana travels much the same route to success and damnation as his predecessor Tony Camonte: he falls in love with the mistress of his mobster boss; he robs his boss of woman, status, and finally of life; he is also incestuously inclined towards his sister Gina, who becomes romantically entangled with Montana's best friend and partner. Montana kills him in a fit of jealous outrage, thus earning the murderous hatred of Gina. Finally he meets his doom surrounded by gunmen sent by a rival mobster after Tony has proved himself unable to kill a crime-busting politician.

Many of the scenes in De Palma's film are very closely inspired by their equivalent in the original – some are almost lifted intact – although the dark wit of the earlier film is somewhat lacking. What differences there are can largely be attributed to changes in society and in film censorship. With his Cuban background and his involvement with criminal connections in Colombia, Tony's rise to power is placed within a more explicitly political context. And Prohibition being no more, his wealth and power are derived not from booze but from narcotics; interestingly, whereas Hawks' hero only produced and marketed booze, and never touched it himself, De Palma's mobster not only trades in cocaine but also becomes an addict.

Other differences center around the relaxation of screen

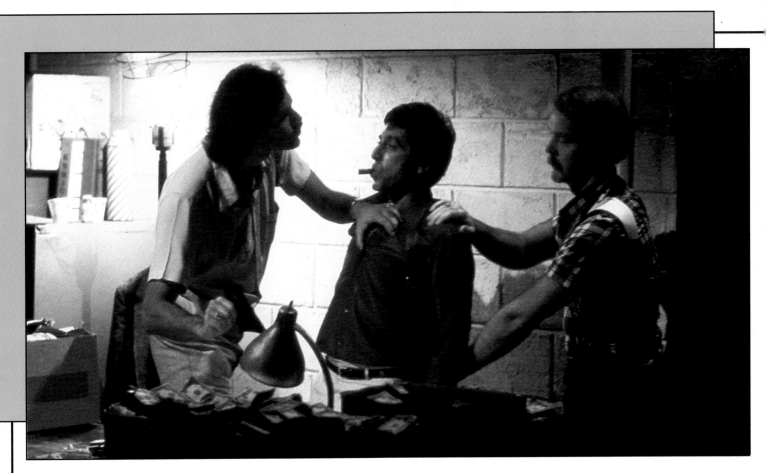

censorship. Montana and his comrades in crime are amazingly foul-mouthed, with four-letter words making up a huge proportion of the dialogue (Montana's mistress at one point even asks him why he has to swear so very much). And the violence is far more gory and explicit than was possible in the Thirties: the first real confrontation involves Tony's friend being hacked up with a chainsaw before his very eyes, and the last – with Tony at the center of a storm of bullets as the Mob's armed forces burst into his mansion – must be one of the longest, bloodiest gunfights in the history of the genre. Even at this climactic point, however, De Palma stays with Hawks' ironic conception of gross ambition run disastrously wild: the camera, surveying the carnage, tracks from Tony's dead body to a neon sign stating "The World Is Yours."

Eastwood and Reynolds
This awareness of the classic crime movies, which lies somewhere between homage and parody, permeates all the recent gangster films. Most blatantly and broadly parodic is **City Heat** (1984), which stars Clint Eastwood as cool cop Speer and Burt Reynolds as seedy shamus Mike Murphy. Set in Kansas City in 1933 – a thriving cattle-town thrown wide open to the Mob, who run its bordellos, gambling joints and jazz dives – the film sees the heroic pair put aside the rivalry that has dogged them since Murphy left the Department to become a private gumshoe, and take on the gangs led by mobsters Primo Pitt (Rip Torn) and Leon Coll (Tony Lo Bianco).

Many of the movie's elements are reminiscent of earlier films: the event that brings about the pair's crusade against the gangsters is the murder of Murphy's none-too-honest partner Dehl Swift (Richard Roundtree) – echoes of Sam Spade's motives in **The Maltese Falcon**. A key witness (Irene Cara) is menaced by the mob while leaving a cinema – the location for Dillinger's death at the hands of the FBI. A massive shoot-out between the Law and the Mob takes place in a cavernous garage owned by Pitt – bringing back memories of the

dreadful St Valentine's Day Massacre.

What makes the film so enjoyable, however, is the way it combines its pastiche of both gangster films and private-eye movies with a lively comic tone, built around snappy, absurd one-liners (Coll threatens, "Cross me and you're snail food"), and an amiable sense of self-parody regarding Eastwood's and Reynolds' movie-images.

Eastwood in particular is admirably tongue-in-cheek, taking his customary cool and heroic efficiency to enjoyably ludicrous extremes: at one point he strides slowly but steadily into a massive gunfight that has been raging for minutes on end without anyone getting killed, and carefully, miraculously disposes of each mobster with a single, expertly aimed bullet.

Full-scale nostalgia
Even though, with its dark and rainy backstreets, seedy offices and gaudy cat-houses, **City Heat** is a good-looking film, it relies for effect more on its generally comic situation and themes than on stunning set-design and knowing reference. Francis Ford Coppola's **The Cotton Club** (1984), however, takes the opposite tack and mounts a full-scale nostalgic re-creation of the Gangster Era through a number of characters drawn from real-life (Dutch Schultz, Lucky Luciano, Owney Madden – not to mention film-stars like Chaplin, Cagney and Gloria Swanson) and through a stylistic rehash of motifs from the archetypal movie genres of the period – the gangster film itself and the musical. Set for much of its length in Harlem's legendary Cotton Club – a ritzy night-club patronized by fashionable and wealthy whites – the film charts not only the twists and turns in the gang-warfare blighting Harlem during and just after Prohibition, but also the dangerous love-triangle that develops between cornettist Dixie Dwyer (Richard Gere), dancer Vera Cicero (Diane Lane) and mobster Schultz (James Remar).

This romantic aspect of the generally thin plot is somewhat over-familiar, a tame reworking of an age-old story used in only slightly different form in **Little Caesar** (Rico becoming jealous

Scarface (1983).
Left: Tony Montana at the height of his powers in Brian De Palma's **Scarface** (1983), relaxing in a Miami nightclub with corrupt cops. Before long however his dream will turn into a nightmarish bloodbath.

Far left: Tony Montana (Al Pacino) chomps on a cigar to soothe his nerves during a tense moment.

City Heat (1984).
Below: Lieutenant Speer (Clint Eastwood) and former cop-turned-private eye Mike Murphy (Burt Reynolds) swapping insults.

Bottom: Eastwood playing the all-powerful policeman able to outwit and kill a whole streetful of gun-crazy hoodlums.

The Cotton Club (1984).
Far right: Dutch Schultz (James Remar) points an accusing finger at Vincent Dwyer (Nicholas Cage) backstage at *The Cotton Club*.

Right: Jealousy aroused and pride battered, Dutch Schultz (James Remar) displays his disturbingly vicious temper.

Bottom: Prohibition passion: Dixie Dwyer (Richard Gere) falls in love with Vera Cicero (Diane Lane) – who just happens to be the moll of psychotic Dutch Schultz, gang-boss of Harlem. The story of young love standing up against tyrannical jealousy is as old as the mobster genre itself.

when Joe Massara gets involved with a cabaret dancer) and in **Scarface** (Camonte/Montana becoming enraged when his sister goes off with his best friend).

It's a weak hook on which to hang the movement of the film's story, since it is quite clear from the very beginning that Dixie will eventually stand up, find courage, and tell Schultz to leave the girl who loves him alone. Far more interesting is the backdrop of gang-rivalries that is the reason for the film's period setting.

Harlem mobsters
In reality, Dutch Schultz was a ruthless racketeer who moved into Harlem to take over the illegal numbers games. Owney Madden was the British-born figure who owned the Cotton Club, and became friend and partner to some of the most notorious criminals in New York; he prided himself not only on his successful club, which offered amongst its musical delights artistes like Duke Ellington and Cab Calloway, but also on his high-quality bootleg beer.

Madden became close to top mafioso Lucky Luciano, a truly dangerous mobster who took a dislike to Schultz when it was rumored that the Dutchman planned to murder Thomas Dewey, a successful investigator of organized crime who soon afterwards would manage to put Luciano behind bars. Afraid that killing Dewey would bring increased "heat" down on the New York underworld, Luciano decided that the Dutchman had to go: in 1935 Schultz and three henchmen were brutally murdered in a New Jersey restaurant by a lone Syndicate hit-man.

These complex and fascinating real-life intrigues are sown with expert ease into the wider fabric of **The Cotton Club**'s story. The mobsters, unlike the romantic couple of Dixie and Vera, are portrayed with vivid color and energy: Remar is admirably vicious and thuggish as Schultz; Bob Hoskins is charismatic, canny and deeply likeable as Madden, always trying to keep the peace between Schultz and his rivals; Joe

Dallesandro makes a marvelously sinister and suave appearance as Luciano, quietly planning Schultz's demise.

Other figures, while fictional, are also clearly based on real-life characters. Dixie Dwyer, the companion of hoodlums who moves on to become a Hollywood film-star famed for playing gangsters, is clearly inspired by George Raft, while his brother Vincent Dwyer (Nicholas Cage) adds another echo of reality: in a chaotic shoot-out which is intended to kill Schultz's sideman Sol Weinstein (Julian Beck in a marvelously nasty role) but actually results in the death of several innocent children, Vincent becomes known as "Mad Dog", a name that firmly aligns him with real-life hoodlum Vincent "Mad Dog" Coll.

The Cotton Club presents a detailed, atmospheric portrait of organized crime's operations in New York in the late Twenties and early Thirties, blending fact and fiction with ease. But for all its style (much of the film is deliberately shot with the panache and quick-fire techniques of the original Thirties movies), it remains to some extent a glossy, glamorous confection that never comes up to the standards set by Coppola's earlier **Godfather** epics. It is a film that works well on the surface, but never manages to portray any real emotional depth or sense of danger; it also never even attempts to analyze the power struggles at play, but simply depicts them.

Pinnacle of a genre
For a gangster movie that combines an entertaining story, vivid style and interesting ideas, we must turn to a work which mixes the strengths of the genre-film with those of the more serious "art-movie": **Once Upon a Time in America.**

Leone's film deals with the lives and times of a group of Jewish gangsters (there is nothing perverse in their being Jewish; the criminal fraternity has never consisted solely of Italians, and during the Twenties many cities – especially New York – included very large Jewish contingents among their criminal fraternity). The story extends from the gang's sordid

Far left: The heavily guarded portals of the Federal Reserve Bank in Manhattan, target for Max's planned robbery which brings about Noodles' betrayal of his old friends, in **Once Upon a Time in America** (1984).

The Cotton Club (1984).
Left: Dutch Schultz (James Remar) makes a few cutting remarks to rival hoodlum Joe Flynn (John Ryan) at a party while Frenchy Demange (Fred Gwynne), manager of *The Cotton Club,* looks on.

Below: Doin' the Cotton Club Stomp. The excellent tap-dancing talents of Sandman and Clay Williams (Gregory and Maurice Hines) in one of the many delightful dance sequences.

boyhood experiences on the Lower East Side in 1922, through the last few months of Prohibition in the early Thirties, to 1968 when, it seems, only one of the gang, David "Noodles" Aaronson (Robert De Niro) is left alive.

In superficial description, the film might sound like a conventional series of gangster scenes: speakeasy parties, armed robberies, shoot-outs between rival gangs, whorehouse revelries, and romance in ritzy restaurants. But Leone, who had already created what is perhaps the definitive modern Western with **Once Upon a Time in the West** (1968), wanted to do something different. What marks the film out as special is the way its whole tone and meaning hinges on a crucial moment of change in Noodles' life: the dark and rainy night when, to prevent his partner Max (James Woods) from attempting a risky bank-robbery (which Noodles feels is sure to end in the demise of the gang), he informs the police of the gang's plans.

This well-meaning act of betrayal results, it seems, in the deaths of Noodles' three fellow gang-members, and after visiting an opium den in Chinatown to blot out his memory of the disaster, Noodles takes a train, at random, to Buffalo where for 35 years he will lead a quiet, anonymous life in hiding, away from the vengeance of Max's enraged friends.

Only in 1968 does the guilt-ridden old man return to the land of the living, a saddened ghost haunted by the nightmare of his telephone call to Sergeant Halloran. Summoned to New York by a mysterious letter, he finally discovers that it was not he but Max who betrayed the gang, who set up the fatal robbery in order that, believed dead, he could flee with the gang's accumulated fortune and assume a new identity: that of a man now known, in the Sixties, as Secretary Bailey, a politician charged with corrupt labor practices.

Contemporary myth

Leone's film is epic, in length, period detail and visual style. Rarely has the look of a period film been so accurate and yet so mythological in effect; it is like a collective dream, fueled by memories of countless classic gangster movies, brought to vivid life. The story, too, is epic, tracing the escalation in power and violence of the gang's exploits, from boyish petty crime, through bootlegging, to an involvement in political intrigue with the Teamsters' union. The film is full of memorable, superbly staged and often violent scenes: a daring jewel robbery; a transport union official (Treat Williams) soaked in petrol and menaced with a lighted match; an opulent drunken speakeasy party where a casket bearing the inscription "Prohibition" is laid to rest. But this epic tone in counterbalanced by a more intimate concern with Noodles' sense of guilt and failure.

The subject of the film as it progresses becomes less a nation's history of violence than a meditation on loyalty and betrayal, on wrong choices made, opportunities missed, and lives wasted. Leone himself has rightly identified his film's central character as Time itself: the story is fragmented into associative flashbacks, depicting Noodles' attempts in 1968 to unravel and come to terms with his inglorious past.

Seen through his eyes, crime and violence are not to be celebrated; for him, they are traps that eventually led him to lose his greatest friends, and to spend 35 years of his life locked in private guilt and regret. Leone looks at the archetypal American Dream as expressed in the ambitions of movie gangsters, and finds it wanting: it is a long and melancholy nightmare, encapsulated in the film's opening moments of brutal killings and a fatal telephone call.

Mob reality

Once Upon a Time in America never glamorizes its characters. Noodles, though romantic, loyal and concerned with the idea of fair play, is also deeply, violently distrustful of women (he commits two brutal rapes), and timidly ineffectual when it comes to standing up for his principles in arguments against his friend Max. Max is even less pleasant: devious, a little crazy, sadistic towards women, and all too ready to betray his partners in crime.

These are not the honorable heroes of dynastic splendor seen in **The Godfather**. They start off in their criminal careers as amateur guttersnipes, and although they will become more violent and powerful, they will never attain real "class". Only Max will escape from the low-life into the big-time, because he alone is unscrupulous and devious enough to be assured of a place in politics.

And yet for all his failings, Noodles finally, in old age, achieves some sort of dignity. Invited to a party given by the Secretary who, as Max, betrayed him so many years before, Noodles is asked by his old friend to kill him; Max sees the only way out from scandal surrounding his political corruption as death. But in discovering at last the truth about the nightmare that has haunted him for more than three decades, Noodles refuses to take up the gun; the old gang, he says, would never have touched such a job.

In an ending bleak, surprising and overwhelmingly moving, Noodles refuses to indulge any desire for revenge, turns his

Once Upon a Time in America
(1984).
Far left: The fatal phone call. David "Noodles" Aaronson returns to his lost empire after 35 years of lonely exile.

Left: Young Max (Rusty Jacobs) is beaten up by a rival neighborhood gang from the Lower East Side.

Above: Body with No Name. Of the three corpses found after the disastrous bank-robbery in 1933, only two are identifiable; the other is black, charred flesh, and signifies the death of demented gangster Max, the birth of Secretary Bailey.

back once and for all on violence, and comes to terms with his fraught past. He now knows that his belief that he betrayed his friends back in 1933 was an illusion, that he was not the culprit but the victim; and yet he is now able to live with his memories, with the knowledge of his wasted life. In so doing, he once more assumes control of his own destiny.

European influence
It is perhaps not surprising that it takes a European director working in an American genre to deliver the most profound gangster film of the Eighties so far. It is possibly no coincidence that other Europeans – John Boorman with **Point Blank**, Louis Malle with **Atlantic City** – also dealt with the gangster film in terms of Time and Memory. Coming from overseas, these directors have been able to some extent to stand outside the traditions of the gangster film and use them for their own artistic purposes.

Once Upon a Time in America is full of ideas and emotion, and also entertaining. It has an awareness of the films that preceded it, and yet never simply rehashes past successes. In employing the conventions of the gangster film it breaks new ground, constructing a strangely somber, wistful and ironic portrait of the American Dream, concerned both with the nation in general and one man's inner emotions in particular. From its superb performances to its vivid photography, from its complex script to its careful use of music (even the Beatles' "Yesterday" is aptly pressed into service, outlining Noodles' sad feelings of loss and waste), its four hours constitute a masterpiece of the gangster genre.

It is a perfect example of what contemporary film-makers can achieve with a genre that is still fertile after more than 50 years. With **Once Upon a Time in America** leading a field of interesting, ambitious and resolutely modern movies, the gangster film is assured of a healthy future indeed.

PICTURE CREDITS

Marlon Brando has his cuts
examined in **On the Waterfront**
(1954).